the Perot LEGACY

A New Political Path

PAT BENJAMIN

Donna Donovan, Editor

NEW YORK

LONDON • NASHVILLE • MELBOURNE • VANCOUVER

the Perot LEGACY
A New Political Path

Published in New York, New York, by Morgan James Publishing. Morgan James is a trademark of Morgan James, LLC. www.MorganJamesPublishing.com

ISBN 978-1-61448-472-1 paperback
Library of Congress Control Number: 2012954970

Cover Design by:
Rachel Lopez
www.r2cdesign.com

Interior Design by:
Bonnie Bushman
The Whole Caboodle Graphic Design

Morgan James is a proud partner of Habitat for Humanity Peninsula and Greater Williamsburg. Partners in building since 2006.

Get involved today! Visit
www.MorganJamesBuilds.com

When the government fears the people, there is liberty.
When the people fear the government, there is tyranny.
—Thomas Jefferson

Dedication

This book is dedicated to those people who were committed in their hearts, minds, and through their many activities, to the successful completion of our mission. These are some of the people who, unfortunately, did not live to complete the full experience or continue the fight. They include Lily Andrews from Maine, Paul Truax from Texas, John Moore from New Jersey, John Morehart from New Jersey, Frank Conrad from New Jersey, Rosemary Deal from New Jersey, and Jim Callis from Arizonia.

Contents

Acknowledgements

Without the time, support, inspiration, and contributions of the people featured in this book, the full story could never have been written. These people include: Diane McKelvey and her husband Alec, Donna Donovan (researcher, content and copy editor of this book), Jim Mangia, Beverly Kidder, Paul and Donna Truax, Marilyn Tighe, Scott Sanders, Tim Shaw, Bob Davidson, Shar Johnson and her daughter Heather, Elizabeth Christman Danforth, Pauline Kline, Judy Duffy, Ralph Perkins, Nikki Love, Deanna Clapsadle (De), Mike Hicks, Mark Sturdevant, Russ Verney, Dean Barkley, Dorothy and Herb Drew, Beverly Kennedy, Gerry Moan, and Pat Choate.

Along with these people, others who helped to keep the Perot-inspired political reform movement alive and growing have included, Matt Sawyer, Mike Morris, Tom McLaughlin, Dale Welch Barlow, Dror Bar-Sadeh, Melanie Carne, CJ Barthelingi, Norris Clark, and many others too numerous to list. In fact, it took tens of thousands of volunteers willing to commit both time and money to keep the mission moving forward. And, it took a leader like Ross Perot to encourage and support us all.

Finally, I have to thank my close friends Roz Davis and Diana Stark, as well as my husband , Milton Benjamin, for their patience and encouragement throughout the process of setting the record straight.

Author's Notes

What qualifies me to address these issues and problems?

During the 1960s, I earned a Bachelor's degree in history and political science from Wayne State University in Detroit Michigan. I followed this with a Master's degree in history from New York City-based Columbia University, concentrating on Russian Studies and twentieth century Soviet Communism.

I've been a political activist since the late 1950s, first working in the Martin Luther King wing of the Civil Rights movement, followed in the late 1960s with involvement in the moderate faction of the Feminist movement, supporting equal pay for equal work.

By 1975, I saw both the Feminist and Civil Rights movements getting bogged down in single-issue battles – abortion and affirmative action respectively. That's when I decided to take a "hiatus" from active political involvement.

Between 1979 and 1992, I started two companies, and experienced the highs and lows of entrepreneurship, and the corruption of the political and corporate systems.

In 1992, Ross Perot appeared on the scene. He was saying things about our government, economy, and society that I had personally experienced. He was — and still is — a down-to-earth charismatic billionaire who is a man of the people.

Talk shows, magazines, newspapers, the Internet, lectures, and books by reporters and professors have addressed the Perot phenomenon. My focus has also included the people who were drawn to Ross Perot's message, and who became actively involved in bringing his message to every American – a mission we all still share to this day, in 2012.

In 1997, I was elected National Vice Chair of the Reform Party, which provided the incredible opportunity for me to experience this movement, both as a volunteer answering telephones and working in the trenches, and as a state and national leader.

Because of these experiences, I feel qualified — and obligated — to present the truth I experienced as an "insider," and to share the views of other involved activists. I'm able to tell the story from these volunteer activists' perspective. That's what drove me to write this book addressing the people involved and the issues, as well as the impact on our political system since the 1990s through 2012.

My forty-plus years of experience as an on-the-ground political activist in several political movements, along with my academic credentials, gave me a well-suited background to write this book.

Sadly, we were poorly and sometimes brutally treated by the political establishment in the 1990s. That disdain and dismissiveness is even stronger in 2012. Politics has become nastier and way too expensive for the average person to even entertain getting involved by running for office. Reform is critically needed, and I hope this book helps motivate the American people to join forces to continue the fight that Ross Perot and his activist volunteers began in 1992.

Prologue

An enormous trade and budget deficit, a continually growing government debt, outsourcing of American jobs, and elected representatives who don't listen to the people who put them in office and pay their salaries.

All of these issues are major problems today in the United States. In fact, these problems have grown worse since they were first discussed by Ross Perot in his 1992 campaign for President of the United States.

I have come to believe, as have many of the other activists who began their political journeys in the 1992 Perot campaign for president that real changes are needed, and can only be made by the people's direct involvement in the running of their government.

Today, in 2012, there is a building momentum for reclaiming our country using a different kind of politics. A number of new organizations have recently formed, modeled after the Perot-founded issues organization United We Stand America (UWSA). One of these groups is called No Labels, which (like UWSA) is made up of Democrats, Independents, Republicans and alternative party activists. Their goal is to break the gridlock in Congress by getting the American people involved, and pushing their elected representatives to begin solving problems instead of ignoring or making them worse.

A positive change in government can be made. What does it take?

Voting by millions, telephone calls, e-mails, letters, and petitions to our local, county, state and federal representatives, as well as massive demonstrations by the people in front of our nation's capital, Washington DC.

In order to succeed, we also need to understand what the Democrats and Republicans in our current two-party political system have done in the past to squelch any attempts to change the political structure.

This is the story of a citizen-action movement that turned ordinary citizens into street fighters, taking them into the depths of dirty politics that they had no idea existed. It exposes the back-room deals, intimidation, stalkers, and death threats experienced by many of the millions of people inspired by Ross Perot's 1992 and 1996 campaigns for the presidency.

Also addressed is how these 1990s political activists - as young as 14 at the time - have evolved politically over the last 20 years – including what drove them to get involved, and what's important to them today.

I continue to be convinced that "We the People," working together, can accomplish this mission. To keep democracy alive, the economy growing, and our government honest and truly representing the American people, it's time to turn the message into action and take back control of our country.

Chapter 1

The Movement

I answered the telephone and a voice said, "You should have burned in the ovens in World War II." A recurring nightmare? Yes. But also part of my reality in the 1990s.

This reality is one of the reasons I need to set the record straight. In December 2005, I made a decision about how to spend the next stage of my life. I decided to write a book about the millions of citizen activists in the United States, including me, who joined an unprecedented political movement in 1992. The overwhelming evidence that the United States government wasn't listening to its citizens drove us to act on our anger and frustration.

Just as I made this decision, I received a call at my home in Cherry Hill, New Jersey from a Connecticut friend, Donna Donovan, whom I had met in that 1990s political reform movement. Donna proceeded to tell me a story that reinforced my decision. She said, "Yesterday I was on my way to a garage to service my car. While I was driving, another car passed. The driver honked at me, smiled, and gave me a thumbs-up sign. It wasn't the first time this had happened." Donna continued, "I have a bumper sticker on my car's rear window that says 'Ross Was Right.' Recently I realized people had begun reacting strongly and positively to this message. When I arrived at the service station and pulled in, one of the mechanics had an amazing reaction. With tears in his eyes, the mechanic looked at my bumper sticker and said, 'Where is he? We need him now more than ever.'"

The "he" to whom the mechanic was referring, named on the bumper sticker, was Ross Perot—the man who represented truth, trust, and hope to many Americans. The man who founded and led our political reform movement, creating a new political path.

Who is Ross Perot?

Ross Perot, born in Texarkana, Texas, is the son of a cotton broker. He grew up during the Depression in a $4,000 house. After high school, he received an appointment to the U.S. Naval Academy. Ross served on the USS Sigourney and the USS Leyte in the 1950s. In his book *My Life & The Principles of Success*, he explained,

> One day while I was on the bridge of the Leyte, working as assistant navigator, Stan Farwel an IBM executive ... came over and said, "Son would you be interested in a job with IBM?" ... I looked at him and said: "Mr. Farwell, I am twenty-six years old. I've worked since I was six years old, and I always had to look for work. You are the first person in my life who has ever offered me a job. You bet I would like to have an interview with your company, IBM, and I don't even know what you do." [Farwell] broke out laughing, and said "You don't know what IBM does?" I said, "Well we have IBM typewriters on the ship." He said, "No Ross, I'm interested in you because the captain tells me that you have a lot of knowledge about the gunfire control computers, and we are in the computer business." P. 66

In 1957, Ross Perot joined IBM, and as he says, the rest is history. In the 1960s, Ross Perot left IBM and founded Electronic Data Systems (EDS). He surrounded himself "with people who were far more talented and gifted than I was" —one of the secrets to his success.

Today billionaire Ross Perot has changed a lot from that young man who founded EDS. However, he still retains the basic east Texas values of compassion, patriotism, and hard work. He is a man who became a billionaire and wanted to give back to the people and the country where he was given the chance to succeed.

Ross Perot contributes to many worthy causes, such as medical research and hospitals, the majority of which is done under the radar of the media. In particular, Ross supports our military and helps thousands of United States Army, Air Force, Navy, and Marine veterans.

However, the part of Ross Perot's legacy that has impacted millions of Americans and gained him the most visibility is his direct involvement in politics. In 1992, Ross Perot ran for president as an independent. In 1996, he ran as the candidate of the state Reform Parties. He funded the issues organization United We Stand America, and contributed to the organization of a citizens' group to help with emergency preparedness after September 11, 2001.

Many Americans believe the legacy that will outlast Ross Perot is his initiative to put the control of this country's government back into the hands of its people.

Involved reformers speak

Numerous books have been written about Ross Perot. These books explore his personal and business lives, as well as the political impact of his 1992 presidential campaign and the resulting creation of the Reform Party. However, so far, this is the only book that has been written by a citizen volunteer *participant* in the daily activities of the 1992 Ross Perot presidential campaign, United We Stand America (UWSA), the Reform Party (RPUSA), and the post-9/11 emergency preparedness network (named United We Stand, UWS) following September 11, 2001. For the first time, you will hear my and others' reasons for involvement in the government and political reform movement inspired and invigorated by Ross Perot. Some of us were political activists who were reenergized by him. But many were people who had never participated in politics and were transformed by Perot and the reform movement into politically involved Americans.

Movement goals

The goal of this political movement was not and is not just to create a third party. An alternate party, like the Reform Party, is just one way citizens can have an impact on their government. Some people choose to join citizen action groups or local activist organizations. Some even choose to run for office.

Millions of people were and still are drawn to the movement by the issues that Ross Perot addressed. In 1992, many of his issues were not even on the radar screen for either major political party. Yet his campaign's emphasis on issues such as trade, the growing national debt and deficit, and campaign reform resonated so loudly that almost twenty million Americans cast their votes for independent Perot in November 1992. And today, the trend toward independent voting continues to increase. As observed in the book *The 100 Best Trends 2006* by George Ochoa and Melinda Corey, "According to the Harris Poll, 24% of Americans call themselves independents." This and other findings suggest that independents are the fastest growing political constituency in the United States.

The main emphasis of this movement, from the beginning, has been—and still is—the need for the people's direct involvement in the governing of the United States of America, in order to make sure every change is good for the country and its people. Also, as Ross Perot often said, "Never ask yourself, 'Is it legal or illegal?' Simply ask yourself as a leader, 'Is it right or wrong?' If it's wrong, don't do it" (address to the graduating class of Port Huron High School, 6/7/ 1995).

Bias and disagreement

In this book, I have chronicled the political and life-changing events experienced not just through my own eyes, but also through the eyes of some others who signed on to the Perot campaign and the subsequent political movement. These people represent the thousands of voters I have spoken to since 1992. They had and have many different professions. They live in every part of the United States. Yet, they have shared the same political environment—the Perot-inspired reform movement, which began in 1992 and is still having an impact today.

Within the movement, from the beginning, participants didn't always agree with one another on every topic. Yet, for a time, we were able to overcome these differences because we did agree on our core values and our primary mission. The problems with today's politics include the hardening of political positions in both of the major political parties, the growing representation of extremist views, and the unwillingness to compromise. These problems have made passing laws and effectively and democratically governing more and more difficult.

In our political reform movement, we chose to set aside social policy—such as abortion and gun control—and focus on political and economic reform. Today in politics, it's more obvious than ever that the greater emphasis is on social issues that divide people, rather than on the core issues and values that bring them together. Overall, our activist supporters represent the moderate or middle positions on the core political and economic issues.

A variety of members

It's important to note that the Perot constituency varied from Perot's independent campaign for president to United We Stand America (UWSA) and later the Reform Party. In 1992, people supported Ross Perot based on his stance on issues; their trust in him; his clear, direct, outspoken statements; and their desire to have him run for president. In 1993, we who continued in the Perot-inspired reform movement as part of the issues organization UWSA were focused on educating elected officials and the public. We elected to reform the system through an indirect process, rather than by running our own candidates.

In fact, following a line-by-line comparison of the Republican "Contract With America" with the "Principles of Reform" developed during the early Perot movement, both Russ Verney and Donna Donovan concluded that the GOP position statement was inspired by and based in part on our document.

Then, in 1995–96, a democratic vote of the UWSA members led to a decision to convert to a political party—the Reform Party. With that change, many activist supporters who had left after 1992 because they wanted to create their own political party and run their own candidates returned to the fold. Also, we added new third-party supporters. Unlike in 1992, numerous events occurred that limited Ross Perot's voting numbers as a presidential candidate in 1996, not the least of which was his exclusion from the presidential debates by the Republican and Democratic presidential candidates and the "private" bipartisan (not nonpartisan) Commission on Presidential Debates.

In fact, after 1996, external and internal events and circumstances, which are detailed in later chapters, continued to contribute to the diminished size and impact of the Reform Party following the chaotic 2000 Reform Party National Convention. Some people in the movement remained in the party. Others ran for elected office at local, state, and national levels as independents, third-party candidates, or as members of the two major parties. Still others joined issues organizations, faith-based groups, and many other volunteer associations in efforts to maintain our freedom, promote our democracy, and to help our citizens in any number of ways.

Overview

Through the voices of participants, this book presents the start, the development, and the continuation of Ross Perot's legacy—citizen involvement in politics and the governing of our country. Here, the reform movement's participants address the many forms of vigilance they adopted and encouraged to preserve our democracy and freedom by answering Ross Perot's key question—"Is it good for the country?" *The Perot Legacy: A New Political Path* explores how each American, by reaching out to other Americans, can play a role in running our government. This book encourages all of us to use every means possible to "take our country back."

Chapter 2

The Campaign

"These are the best of times. These are the worst of times."

Those words by Charles Dickens in *A Tale of Two Cities* perfectly describe the state of American politics over the last two decades. It was the best of times because Americans began to wake up and eventually rise up in 1992. They slowly began to realize it was time to move from the political status of "outsider" to their legitimate position of "insider." It was the worst of times because political party members had been ideologically moving further away from one another, within each party as well as between political parties. In fact, extremists in both parties were beginning to move into positions of power.

The pull-and-tug of extremes seemed to be greater in the Republican Party. In a 1992 article for Scripps-Howard News Service, Jane Lowey reported, "Several leading GOP moderates ... recently announced the formation of the Republican Majority Coalition, a national organization 'to take our party back' from the Religious Right. The organization made the stand clear in its following Statement of Purpose: 'We believe issues such as abortion, mandatory school prayer, homosexuality, the teachings of creationism and other similar questions recently inserted into the political context should instead be left to the conscience of individuals.'"

The missing link

People across America were feeling the tension—and often disenfranchisement— of the polarization within the two major parties. And then the missing link that completed the chain fell into place. That chain united millions across America. There are many stories behind the people who became part of this chain of political awakening. I was one of those people.

For me, the key to the discovery of that missing link came from my son Steven. One spring day in 1992, Steven walked into the house where we lived in East Brunswick, New Jersey, and said, "I just signed a petition."

"For what?" I asked.

"To put Ross Perot on the ballot for president of the United States."

I replied, "Who's Ross Perot?"

For me, that was the beginning of fifteen years of the "best of times" and the "worst of times."

For Diane McKelvey, from Colon, Michigan, the discovery of Ross Perot—the missing link—also centered on a family member: her husband, Alec. According to Diane, while watching TV, "Alec would thump on the arms of the couch complaining about what the politicians were saying. Alec often said he was glad when Congress recessed because then they would not be spending any more of our money."

Meanwhile, Diane was busy training her racehorses when one of the other trainers at the Marshall, Michigan, fairgrounds said to her, "What do you think of that millionaire guy who's going to run for president?" referring to Ross Perot. At home, Alec kept talking about Perot and told Diane that Mr. Perot was going to be on *Larry King Live*. Diane said, "I decided to watch the show and find out for myself what the fuss was about. To put it mildly, I was astounded by what I saw and heard. No one, absolutely no one, had spoken or addressed issues like he did."

Diane volunteered to work with the Michigan Perot for President campaign. She was asked to carry a petition and get signatures to put Perot on the ballot in Michigan. Diane said, "Amazing to me, every person I presented the petition to signed it! It took no time out of my busy day."

Once her petition was filled with signatures, she took it to the neighboring town where the Perot for President office was located. Diane said, "What I saw there was unbelievable! They had a sign out on the highway saying 'Sign Perot petitions here,' and a table set up with several people and petitions. Cars were stopping and people were walking across this busy highway to sign them! The groundswell I saw was simply amazing. People really cared."

The groundswell

While Diane was reacting in Michigan, Marilyn Tighe from San Diego, California, became a Perot for President campaign volunteer working the telephones. Marilyn eventually became the office manager "putting out fires, placing volunteers where they were needed. In the beginning we were in someone else's offices then we moved twice to larger quarters. The volunteers were wonderful. Nobody knew anybody, didn't know nor did it matter if they were a Democrat or Republican or other, didn't know their religion, education. He who could, did, he who had, gave. It was wonderful getting an impossible job done."

Meanwhile, back in New Jersey, a sixteen-year-old high school student, Scott Sanders, who couldn't drive or vote, heard about Perot from his excited father. Scott said of his dad, "Politics was a common topic, and he didn't have a whole lot of love for people in office. I picked up on my dad's excitement and did some research."

Scott remembers one phrase in particular. "I believe Perot was asked in one interview what could be done to fix the country and the path on which it was headed. 'Look in the mirror' was the response [from Perot]. Indeed I did." The fire of political reform now burned inside of teenager Scott Sanders.

At the same time Scott awoke politically in New Jersey, Bev Kidder was being introduced to the name Ross Perot. She "ran into a guy at a 'Stop the Toll Roads' rally to end the toll roads in New Jersey. He was wearing a Perot button. I had heard of Ross Perot from my husband who [like Perot] attended Annapolis. I liked what I heard."

Then Bev received a call to attend a meeting being held in a huge lunchroom at a local office building. "Hundreds of people [showed up] and a voice said, 'But there's no one for Princeton.'" Bev volunteered because she lived in Princeton. Bev and one other woman set up a card table near a busy road with a sign on it that said "Perot Petition."

According to Bev, "It was unbelievable. Almost a mob scene. It was the beginning of drive-by signatures. People would drive up and the passenger would get out to sign. The same car would go around the block and they would switch seats and the other person would sign. We were causing a traffic jam, so the police showed up to direct cars ... It proved to me that the people were hungry for a change."

These were the people Ross Perot called his "road scholars." They were on the road to citizen participation in government and political reform in New Jersey, Michigan, and many other states.

Bev remembers, "And then the reporters showed up ... The Trenton Times, The Trentonian, The Associated Press, The New York Times ... all asking me the same questions:

INTERVIEWER: Why do you support Ross Perot?

BEV KIDDER: Because neither party represents me. Each party has been taken over by extreme elements. There is a huge political vacuum in the center.

INTERVIEWER: What do you mean by "vacuum?"

BEV:	The Republicans are too far right and the Democrats are too far left.
INTERVIEWER:	Could you give me an example of that?
BEV:	Okay. The Republicans want to climb into your bedroom and tell you what to do. The Democrats want no personal controls, but they want to take your money. It's pretty simple.
INTERVIEWER:	But isn't Perot just a wealthy businessman?
BEV:	Wasn't Reagan just an actor, and Carter a peanut farmer? I looked at the Constitution and couldn't find anything that says rich people can't run [for office]. That would have eliminated all of the Kennedys."

Bev continued, "Just about every week I got calls from the press asking, 'When is Perot going to announce he's running for president?' The fact was we were passing petitions for a candidate that had not declared.... Finally I said, 'Look, Perot said he would run for president when citizens got him on the ballot in all fifty states. He's not even on the ballot here in New Jersey, because we haven't turned in petitions yet. Later I found out ... Arizona would be the last state to file in September 1992."

While we, the volunteers all over this country, were busy gathering signatures to put Ross Perot's name as a candidate for president on all fifty state ballots, Paul and Donna Truax were responding to Ross Perot's wake-up call in Perot's hometown of Dallas, Texas.

Paul Truax described his introduction to that wake-up call: "The night that Mr. Perot made his covenant with America [on the Larry King show], I was lying flat in bed listening with great attention. When the announcement came, my wife [Donna] said that she didn't know it was possible for a fifty-four-year-old man in a prone position to go straight up and levitate for a full thirty seconds while shouting 'hallelujah!' all at the same time."

Shortly after that, Donna Truax, Paul's wife, volunteered at Perot's national campaign headquarters in Dallas, and Paul followed a week later. Paul and Donna were "stunned by the vast assortment of humanity [they] encountered at the Dallas headquarters."

Paul stated, "If you build it, they will come. When Ross Perot made his announcement on Larry King, he started a building process, and they came. Boy, did they come! They came [to Dallas] from every direction and every walk of life. They paid their own way to volunteer in the [Dallas] phone bank because they knew that something was in the air. A sea change was happening in American politics, and they wanted to be part of it. It was a rebirth of a new freedom—freedom from 'politics as usual.' [It was] freedom from the hegemony [domination] of the two major parties."

Paul described those who came to volunteer at the Dallas phone bank as "these peaceful freedom fighters. They were everyone and anyone who could be imagined. Small businessmen and women actually closed down their business to come and volunteer. They were white, brown, yellow, rich, and poor. There was a guy in his fifties with tattoos running up both arms. He was sitting next to a wealthy woman who had just stepped off the society page of the Dallas Morning News. There were people who had never voted and those who voted every time the polls opened. Boys and girls in their teens sat next to men and women who were grandparents. There were liberals and conservatives, and a lot of middle-of-the-roadies. None of that mattered; they were all Americans who had come to take their country back."

According to Paul, the headquarters filled the entire floor of an office building and "there were 180 telephones and no '800' telephone number." At that time, this meant that in order to speak with someone at the national headquarters of the Perot for President campaign, you had to pay for that call yourself. But the calls kept coming. They came from all over America as well as from Americans living abroad in Europe and Asia, from Rome and Paris, to Singapore.

Truax said, "The Perot phenomenon was happening all across the United States and the world.... Ninety percent felt the surge of possibility: for change, for more honesty in politics ... for wanting to serve for the betterment of the country and not to line one's own pocket. Then there was the other 10 percent who called. These were the nuts straight out of the Planter's can! Since it was their time and money, they were treated with courtesy and respect." Paul continued, "Political writers from Washington DC and New York came and shook their heads. They had never seen anything like it before— political volunteers sure, but nothing like the numbers, the enthusiasm, or the cross section of Americans."

When I spoke to Paul in 2006, he believed that the "surge is still standing in the wings." He believed Americans had not changed. "They still want the same thing that they aren't getting from either of the two major parties. The lackluster participation at the polls tells the story. Americans understand straight talk and honesty. They are tired of voting for 'the lesser of two evils.' The Perot-type of phenomenon is bubbling on the back burner just waiting for a leader with financing. If these two things came together tomorrow, the country would explode with the energy of thousands of volunteers and millions of voters."

With all of this enthusiasm across the country, as exemplified by Diane and Alec McKelvey, Donna and Paul Truax, Bev Kidder, and millions of other Americans, plus activism and volunteer commitment to political reform, why didn't Ross Perot win the presidency in 1992?

In the summer of 1992, for many Americans "the worst of times" had begun.

Some people say Perot lost supporters when he publicly questioned whether or not to continue his petition drive in July 1992.

On July 16, 1992, Perot cited "the revitalization of the Democratic Party" and his wish to avoid throwing the election into the House of Representatives, as he discontinued active campaigning (Renshon, p. 53).

Many professional campaign organizers thought the unorthodox campaign techniques—such as dependence on thirty-minute infomercials rather than thirty-second commercials and free time on talk shows such as Larry King, plus lack of organization at national campaign headquarters—caused the problem. Because the support had begun at the grassroots level, these campaign professionals believed the volunteers resented any attempt by "Dallas" (shorthand for campaign headquarters of Perot for President) to give them direction, and chaos had taken over. Curiously, at the same time, many of the volunteers in various states expressed their feeling that the campaign had become too authoritarian and too top-down.

The media speaks

The media, through every conceivable communications outlet, spread conflicting information about Perot's statement across continents and to the American voter. Since Perot had never formally declared his candidacy for president, was he or was he not a candidate for president?

On February 20, 1992, Perot had stated on *Larry King Live* he would run if he were placed on all fifty state presidential ballots. In July 1992, this hadn't yet been accomplished, with twenty-six states' ballot petitions still to complete.

At this point, several Perot for President state headquarters closed, while other state offices continued to function at a reduced level. Confusion reigned among the volunteers who felt jilted. Tears were shed. Questions were asked.

Then, the Perot for President campaign committee formed United We Stand America (UWSA), a new organization. According to CJ Barthelingi, the New Jersey coordinator of the Perot campaign, many UWSA (which was not yet officially a corporation or 501(c)4—a tax-exempt social welfare organization) volunteers then became campaign volunteers and went back to work, with funding continued by Ross Perot, gathering signatures in order to put Perot on the ballot in the remaining twenty-six states. UWSA, as an issues organization, would later (1993–95) play a major role in continuing the political reform movement.

Even with the apparent confusion during the summer of 1992 and the active election campaign supposedly put on hold, state volunteers continued to organize. According to Scott Sanders in New Jersey, just age sixteen at the time, "I met a woman named Mary from Morris County. She was the Morris County chair, and I became her unofficial vice chair. I led some of the local organizing meetings and interacted with lots of [Perot campaign] volunteers."

In Pennsylvania, nineteen-year-old Tim Shaw began to listen to Ross Perot. Tim said, "I liked more and more of what I heard. While on vacation in Ocean City, New Jersey

I bought his book *United We Stand* and became convinced this man was for real ... and that the movement behind him was not just a campaign, but a true movement to take our country back."

In the remaining twenty-six states, volunteers continued to gather signatures to put Ross Perot's name on their states' ballots. In late September 1992, Arizona became the fiftieth and final state to place Perot's name on the ballot as a candidate for president of the United States.

Now that Perot's challenge to the people—placing his name as a presidential contender on all fifty state ballots—had been met, what would be his next move? We didn't have to wait long to find out.

The campaign

On October 1, 1992, Perot said that the volunteers "have asked me to run as a candidate for president of the United States. Jim Stockdale, our vice-presidential candidate, and I are honored to accept their request" (Barta 1993, 318).

This announcement was the spark that re-ignited the flame of citizen activism.

A fourteen-year-old from Hawaii named Nikki Love heard that announcement. She was a ninth grader who "... had never really been involved in politics before (couldn't even vote!) but ... was intrigued by Ross Perot." Nikki said, "I was inspired by his patriotic language and impressed that he was so concerned about the long-term future, passing on the debt to future generations.... On the day he officially entered the race in fall '92, I asked my mother to drive me to the Perot headquarters in downtown Honolulu so I could volunteer! I answered phones, held signs, stuffed envelopes, etc. That was the beginning of my 8 years with Perot/UWSA/RP ... and the beginning of my lifelong passion for government reform, government ethics, and politics/policy in general."

As the fire of excitement began to spread once again, Ross Perot was invited to participate in the presidential debates.

The first debate took place on October 11, 1992. Perot addressed the issues he had been talking about since February. When he was asked about his lack of experience in government he replied, "I don't have any experience in running up a four-trillion-dollar debt" (Barta 1993, 344). (Sadly, this statement, with the amount now more than $9 trillion, still applies today.) Even in high school, Perot had been a cracker-jack debater, and it certainly showed in 1992. A poll conducted by CNN/USA on October 11, 1992, found that of those watching, 47 percent rated Perot the winner, 30 percent voted for Clinton, and 16 percent voted for Bush.

The second presidential debate drew 69.9 million households. This debate used a town-hall format with ordinary Americans asking the questions. The emphasis in this debate was placed on the needs of "We the People." The people won this debate with questions on crime, a poor economy, health insurance, and failing schools (Barta 1993, 344).

The third and last presidential debate was broadcast on October 19, 1992. Perot was questioned about the investigations and dirty tricks frequently used in campaigns. He was also asked about the halt of his campaign in July. He stated, "In terms of the American people's concern about my commitment, I'm here tonight, folks; I never quit supporting you as you put me on the ballot in the other twenty-six states.... And talk about not quitting: I'm spending my money on this campaign.... I put my wallet on the table for you and your children" (Barta 1993, 352).

In his closing statement, Perot said, "Stop letting these folks in the press tell you you're throwing your vote away. You have to start using your own head." He then asked the audience, "Who's the best qualified person up here on the stage to create jobs? You might consider somebody who's created jobs. Who's the best person to manage money? Pick a person who's successfully managed money. Who would you give your pension fund and your savings account to manage? And, who would you ask to be the trustee of your estate and take care of your children if something happened to you? Finally, to you students up there, [gesturing toward the students in the balcony in the live audience] God bless you! I'm doing this for you: I want you to have the American dream. To the American people, I'm doing this because I love you" (Barta 1993, p. 353).

According to the former leader of UWSA and the Reform Party, Russ Verney, "the reason Ross Perot was included in the debates was clearly stated in the Congressional Record when legal counsel and debate coordinator to the 1992 George H. W. Bush campaign Bobby Burchfield testified before a committee of the U.S. House of Representatives." Russ said, "Burchfield indicated that President Bush insisted Ross Perot be included in the debates. In fact, if Mr. Perot had not been included, Mr. Burchfield stated, President Bush would not have participated in the debates at all." Verney's opinion is supported in a report entitled *Deterring Democracy: How the Commission on Presidential Debates Undermines Democracy*, jointly issued by eleven organizations including Judicial Watch, Open Debates, National Voting Rights Institute, and Brennan Center for Justice on August 23, 2004, which quotes Burchfield as saying, "We, the Bush campaign, made it a precondition for the debates that Mr. Perot and Admiral Stockdale be included in the debates" (p.13).

It was clear that the candidates and their campaigns, not the Commission on Presidential Debates, ultimately decided which candidates would participate. The candidates still control the debates in 2012, as they did in 1992 and 1996. And, debate participation by a presidential candidate has a huge impact on a candidate's ability to win an election because millions of people are able to see and directly hear the candidate and his or her positions. The effect of Ross Perot's debate appearance in 1992 was demonstrated seven days after the final debate, when twenty-five thousand people in New Jersey showed their strong support for Ross Perot.

The Flemington rally

Bev Kidder and CJ Barthelingi, from the New Jersey Perot for President campaign, contacted the people in Dallas about holding a rally. The response from Dallas campaign headquarters was to send Jeff Zucker to New Jersey. According to Bev Kidder, Jeff said, "Awful! Just horrible," when he came out to see the Flemington Fairgrounds in New Jersey where the rally was to be held. Jeff was not happy with the choice of the Flemington Fairgrounds as a venue for Perot's appearance in New Jersey.

Bev continued, "The heart of the fairgrounds was a racetrack with bleachers which were partially covered. We had rented the place for the statewide rally for Perot. Our plan was to put the speakers in the bleachers where they had a sound system, and the supporters would stand in the racetrack. We expected a few thousand people. It was planned as an event to fire up the volunteers on October 25, just a few days from the election in November ... Then, we got a call the day before Jeff came that it was to be checked out for a visit by Ross Perot himself. 'This is a security nightmare,' mumbled Jeff as we crawled up and down the bleachers." Bev said, hoping to get a better reaction from Jeff, "Hey, it's got everything; huge speakers, concession stands." But he was still mumbling to himself.

Bev continued, "I tried a different approach, I said, 'and the best part is it only cost us a dollar to rent.' I had heard Perot really liked saving money—that Ross the billionaire bought his suits at discount stores! Jeff laughed at that but then said, 'Look, I can't think that this is a place I could recommend that Mr. Perot could come to.'

Bev said, "Today is Tuesday. We need to turn the whole thing around by Sunday. 'We've got hundreds and hundreds of volunteers [of which I was one!] in this county.' Then Al Bond, who was head of Hunterdon County, commented, 'Just tell us what we need to do.' Jeff went off to wander around some more. 'Well it looks like we won't be getting a visit from Ross,' I said to Al. We agreed that the chances were slim."

But Bev and Al were wrong! On the evening of October 24, "people started showing up early," said Bev. "They had driven all night from upstate New York ... We had stayed in 'Command Central' for two days trying to organize what had started out as a New Jersey State Rally for Perot into a national event.... When we started to move toward the stage [late in the morning on October 25] I knew that this had become a watershed ... a place that would always be measured. Every seat was full. The aisles were full. The racetrack was full. The band was playing and the crowd was chanting. In fact, people were still arriving when the event was over! Luckily the local radio station broadcast his [Perot's] speech live so they could listen in their cars."

Bev continued, "Our usual volunteer bodyguards were there, Kung-fu Pete, Steady Eddie, and a bunch of other too-big Jersey guys, aided by the police, to get us to the stage.

"When I went onto the stage for the first time I saw people painting it blue! It turned out that the television crews setting up had complained that they would get lousy pictures against a white background. So the Flemington volunteers went to a hardware store and bought paint and rollers and within an hour it was blue. The paint was literally not dry when Perot gave his speech.

"When I looked out from the stage, I was amazed. It was a sea of people!

"The racetrack seats held 12,500 people. They were full. The aisles were full. People were hanging off of the bleachers. The racetrack was full. The Chief of Police told us there were at least 25,000 people there.

"Flemington Fairgrounds ... was a place where farmers would show off their livestock. It had barns for cattle and sheep. Hunterdon County was still agricultural in 1992.

"But what had been a sleepy rural county had changed into a sea of political action. The Hunterdon volunteers had worked all night to make us proud.

"When I had gotten to the Fairgrounds at 8:00 a.m. Sunday morning it was cloudy and drizzling with a strong wind blowing. Buses were showing up from Pennsylvania, New York and Connecticut.

"Now it was time to start the event. I was the volunteer Press Secretary. I decided to give the people the news I had just gotten. 'The police have just told me that Highway 31 is jammed from Highway 202 and from the north. All of you who decided to get here early are here. The rest may not ever get here.' And they were left stranded, along with many of the press.

"CJ told me to give the 'long version' of my speech as we seated our volunteer county coordinators on the stage. I had just started when someone in the crowd screamed, 'There's a helicopter!' and pointed right. Like a mass of teeming ants the entire crowd surged right. I'm sure if Perot were looking down he would be smiling.

"By now the crowd was in a frenzy chanting 'We Want Ross' over and over! I kept talking though I'm sure no one heard a word.

"Suddenly the crowd surged right again. A town car had pulled up behind the stage and Ross and his wife Margo got out. Our security volunteers rushed to surround him—and he needed it. Some of the crowd vaulted over the fence and ran toward him. I really wasn't worried about an assassination attempt. If someone had tried it they would have been torn apart limb by limb by the crowd.

"Just as Ross was ascending the stairs, the weather broke. The clouds parted and the sun shown down. I figured it was an omen."

Bev was right. It was an omen. Several more rallies followed the one in Flemington, New Jersey—in Denver, Tampa, Kansas City, Long Beach, and Santa Clara, California. As these rallies continued into the final weekend of the campaign, Perot ran thirty-minute TV infomercials.

Nineteen-year-old Tim Shaw from Pennsylvania said, "I will never forget the last line of the last infomercial. The camera focused on Ross as he said 'and finally, some people may ask, Ross why are you doing this? What do you have to gain? Well, for you young people, I'm doing it for you—because I love you and want you to have the American dream.' I was a young person. Ross was looking right at me and he meant it. You don't have to believe that but I do and had been around his people long enough to know this man was everything he was said to be, truly committed to economic and political reform.... I was proud to support him and proud to be part of that movement, which was grounded in sacrifice for one another."

One infomercial focused on economics and addressed Perot's "attacks on Clinton's Arkansas [economic] record in 'Chicken Feathers, Deep Voodoo, and the American Dream' on ABC and NBC" (Barta 1993, 362).

Perot's emphasis on the economy increased the number of votes he received in the presidential election as indicated in *America's Forgotten Majority: Why the White Working Class Still Matters*, by Roy Teixeira and Joel Rodgers, Basic Books, 2000, Chapter 3. Perot was a credible businessman discussing the economy, and an "outsider" just like the rest of us, as he pointed to the money and power wielded by the Washington "insiders."

Ross Perot's campaign for the presidency in 1992 could not have happened without his "common man" appeal, his wealth, and the widespread support of the American people. Perot was able to demonstrate that every person in a democracy matters, as he and his supporters empowered us all.

However, there was one skill that Ross Perot demonstrated in 1992 that was de-emphasized by the media at best and overlooked at worst—his ability to gather political and economic data and focus in on issues that were affecting the United States in 1992—issues that have an even greater impact today. These issues include the impact of NAFTA (North American Free Trade Agreement) and the outsourcing of American jobs, the increasing trade deficit and national debt, the growth of illegal immigration, rising health care costs with a decrease in individual medical choices, the inadequacy of our schools and our education system in comparison to other countries, the corrupting influence of lobbying and money in politics, (i.e., campaign finance reform), and the need to restructure our election system to enable more people to vote as well as run for political office.

Americans who supported Perot in 1992 (almost 20 percent of those who voted in the presidential election) understood the importance of these concerns. Many of us supported and campaigned for Perot because of the issues he addressed. Speaking for myself, even though I was drawn by his ability to connect with the people, I was most impressed with his political and economic views. It seemed like he had read my mind when I first heard him speak about economic and political reform.

Clearly, I was not the only one with this reaction. Diane, Bev, Scott, Paul, Tim, Nikki, and Marilyn had the same reaction, as did an overwhelming majority of the Perot supporters who participated in the 1992 Perot for President campaign.

When Perot lost the election, coming in third, emotions varied. The reactions of Tim Shaw's parents represented two examples. "My mother felt she threw her vote away, and my Dad was mad—mad at the American people who just did not get it."

Russ Verney, chairman of United We Stand America and the Reform Party, stated, "In 1992, the news media created a consortium to conduct exit polling. People leaving the polls were asked for whom they had voted. Voters who said they voted for Perot were asked, 'If Perot was not in the race would you have voted for Bush or Clinton? ... Voters who responded that they had voted for Bush or Clinton were asked, 'If you thought Perot had a chance of winning, would you have voted for him?'

Russ continued, "The news media did not report asking that last question or the analysis of that question. However, pollster Gordon Black of Gordon Black and Associates [who later became executive director of Harris Interactive], wrote an analysis of the responses to that only unreported question. Gordon Black's analysis concluded that if voters thought Perot could win Perot would have won."

And yet, many Perot supporters saw this election as the beginning, not the end. Several groups went off to build new political parties. Others, like me, focused on staying together to keep our beliefs alive—and we did—as the Perot supporters who helped organize and build the issues organization, United We Stand America.

Chapter 3

United We Stand America— The Beginning

December is usually a month filled with shopping, parties, presents, and lots of colorful lights. In 1992, December found the phone lines to Dallas lit up, too.

Across the United States, thousands of people who had actively supported Ross Perot for president began to hold meetings. Out of these meetings kept coming the same message: we can't stop now!

This message was conveyed again and again to Ross Perot, with the thousands of calls to his office from every state in the United States.

The grassroots continue

In December, like many business people, Mr. Perot usually takes advantage of the quiet holiday period to spend time with his family. But in 1992, phone calls swamped the lines in Dallas so much so that Perot had to add operators to cover the telephones.

Ross Perot got the message loud and clear and replied to America on January 11, 1993.

His answer was the reactivation of United We Stand America (UWSA), incorporated December 14, 1992, now as a nonprofit citizens issues group. The organization had originally been created in July 1992 to finish petitioning to get Perot's name on twenty-six state ballots. In fact, Ross Perot had talked about using this name for a new organization as far back as the 1970s, mentioning this in a 1972 interview in *Look* magazine.

In January 1993, UWSA leaders began a nationwide membership drive, and the millions of people who voted for Ross Perot were offered the opportunity to become founding members of the newly incorporated issues organization for a $15 membership fee.

Turnover

Much of the early months in 1993 were spent signing up new members and building an organizational structure in all fifty states. In addition, turnover in leadership took place, as people interested specifically in election campaigns left because the mission was now focused on issues. The new focus was to educate the people and our elected representatives at the state and national levels.

New people, who Perot had stirred awake, were joining UWSA. Most of these volunteers had never been involved with politics or issues before, and after the 1992 campaign were ready to stay or get involved in the continuing reform movement established by Ross Perot. In addition, we were looking for people who were interested in issues and could act as organizers or administrators as well.

The people begin to organize

One of those issues/organizing people who joined UWSA early was Deanna "De" Clapsadle from Ohio. De said, "I was always talking issues in just about any area that people wanted to discuss. I had done the research, and knew too much for any politicians' tastes."

De stayed on after the campaign and joined UWSA because she "felt there was a chance to educate more people quicker as a group.... Others had a chance to alert us on issues they were watching. It seemed like a way to advance the education of voters on many issues and politician's activities."

She describes the first meeting in Ohio as full of people "who were excited to talk about and hear about 'things' the government was really doing. It was nice seeing so many willing to make the effort and show up."

In Connecticut, Linda Cordero, who was to become the elected state leader of UWSA, will never forget her first meeting. She said, "It was held in a small restaurant in Groton, Connecticut. The meeting was called to watch and hear Ross Perot's official UWSA formation announcement on TV. A few people were invited, but word got around fast. The meeting turned out to be standing room only and everyone was happy and excited."

Diane McKelvey from Michigan also will never forget her first meeting because it changed her life completely. Diane said she had voted for Ross Perot in 1992 "because Ross was right! He had energized me, and millions of people, across this great country. The 'sleeping giant' in the form of the American people had been awakened again and there were things to be done."

When Perot announced the formation of UWSA in January 1993, Diane stated that she "made out a check that night and had my money in the mail first thing in the morning.

Later I was proud of the fact that I had one of the lowest membership numbers in my area. Shortly after that I received notification of a meeting in Kalamazoo, at Western Michigan University. We [Diane and her husband Alec] arrived early for the meeting since we had to drive over 45 miles and we didn't want to be late. When we got there what I saw was a huge surprise. It appeared that everyone had arrived early and the room was packed.

"There must have been more than five hundred people, and some had booths set up selling Perot hats, t-shirts, sweat shirts, calendars and the like."

As the meeting progressed, nominations for congressional district coordinators were made. Diane wanted Alec to speak up and nominate himself. To her surprise, "He stood up all right! He stood up and nominated me!"

Diane and the other nominees were asked to give short speeches about themselves. "I remember clearly what I said that night because I was so motivated by what Ross had instilled in me. I told them a small bit about myself, but then I said, 'No one is here to listen to someone talk about themselves. We are here because something is wrong—wrong with our government and our political system. We are here because we have taken the first steps to do something about it. Politicians' talk and most of the time tell us what we want to hear. But that's as far as it goes. The time has passed for talk. It is time to walk the talk. Let's do it.'"

Diane was elected as the 6th congressional district coordinator and, like many of us, learned on the job. She learned about all of the issues and she organized issue committees "with some teachers that were heading up education reform, an economist working campaign finance reform, and an attorney and a law student working on election and lobbying reform."

Diane also developed speaking skills on television and radio, and found herself welcomed with open arms by her congressional representative, Fred Upton, because she clearly represented a significant number of voters.

As Diane and De demonstrate, one of the interesting phenomena within UWSA was that the skills and ability of people played a larger role in their advancement within the organization than who they knew or how much political clout they might have.

I, myself, am also an example of that politically revolutionary method of advancement. I had walked into New Jersey Perot presidential campaign headquarters in June 1992 and was immediately asked to answer telephone calls. I went through a short training session, but did most of my learning during the heat of the battle or by the "learn-as-you-go" method.

After the election, I was one of the people on the telephone to Dallas. We were asking Perot to help us work together as a force for change in politics. Since I was—and still am—particularly focused on issues, I was overjoyed with the formation and organization of United We Stand America. I felt like I had found a community of friends and family. We agreed on many issues, but differed on some. Just as De had hoped, we began to exchange ideas and learn from one another. For example, issue positions ranged from favoring home schooling to vouchers to charter schools to total support of public schools; from single-payer health care to a completely free-market health care system; and from open immigration to the elimination of illegal immigration to a period of no immigration.

I discovered we were not only a political movement, but also a community of friends and family when I returned from a particularly difficult business trip to Munich, Germany, only to be immediately faced with the news that my husband Milton had a brain tumor.

The support and help from UWSA members given to me began in early March 1993. After leaving an organizational business meeting at UWSA headquarters in Edison, New Jersey, I arrived home to a ringing telephone. It was a member of an emergency medical team at my husband's office. Milton had been working overtime, and a woman cleaning the offices had found him on the floor, incoherent. She immediately called 911. The town's emergency medical team (EMT) came within five minutes and called me. They took my husband to the closest hospital in southern New Jersey. I called UWSA headquarters in central New Jersey and immediately Nick, a racecar driver from South River, New Jersey, came over from UWSA headquarters and drove me to the hospital where Milton had been taken. The original diagnosis, after a CAT scan, was a mass on the brain. The neurologist on duty that night assumed it was cancer. Since the mass was so large, the prognosis did not look good. In fact, the doctor said Milton probably didn't have long to live.

The next morning, a neurosurgeon was brought in on the case, and she scheduled an immediate MRI. The good news was that the mass was diagnosed as a benign tumor, a meningioma. The bad news was its size—like a grapefruit— meaning the tumor had to be removed immediately. The neurosurgeon, Dr. Elizabeth Post, said Milton probably had this tumor for years based on its enormous size.

During this entire traumatic period, the members of UWSA were supportive and constantly checking in, giving us both help and support, just like a family.

Milton had successful surgery, but the tumor returned in 1995, growing until it was eventually sterilized by stereotactic radio surgery (a type of targeted, intense radiation) in 1999.

My years in UWSA and the Reform Party, from 1993 to 2000, gave my husband and me a focus outside of our own problems, and helped us keep going. Many people in the movement stepped up to provide emotional and physical support whenever we needed it. And I know this sense of community and support was also there for many other volunteers.

I spent my time in UWSA organizing people, researching issues, and running projects (as New Jersey state issues team leader, as well as co-county coordinator). I educated the UWSA members, the public, and our elected officials in my local and county areas, as well as in the New Jersey state capitol of Trenton and in Washington DC. I focused on the issues that were important to this country and to its citizens in 1993—issues that are even more critical today.

Like me, many volunteers across this country were living their daily lives, with all their ups and downs. They also were devoting long hours to building UWSA into an issues organization, with millions of members motivated by the opportunity to have a positive impact on our political system.

Chapter 4

The Building of
United We Stand America

The structure of UWSA varied from state to state, depending on each state's political power structure. Most states were organized by congressional district. However, in New Jersey—my home state—many people believed in 1993, and continue to believe today, in 2007, that there were political county "bosses" who influenced or controlled all levels of government, including the state legislature as well as our senators and congressional representatives. Since it was perceived that the political power was based in the twenty-one county organizations, we structured UWSA-NJ using a County Coordinator format.

Along with volunteer congressional district, county, and elected state leaders, there was a UWSA staff person placed by the national office at each state headquarters. In addition, there were five regional UWSA leaders placed by headquarters, and each worked with the states in his or her region. There was also one nationally appointed UWSA staffer for each state and region plus volunteer leaders to run the administrative side of the organization. There were volunteer state issues committee team leaders as well. Then, as time went on and people became more educated about the issues, a volunteer national issues team leader was chosen from the volunteer pool. As I said earlier, the volunteer leaders were chosen based on skill at understanding and developing issues, and educating the public and national elected officials. UWSA's focus was on issues, and the understanding and communication of these issues was facilitated in a number of ways.

The people speak

In Ohio, De Clapsadle was "interested in any issue that involved government control over an area of our lives, including tax dollars," she explains, "so I was into just about everything. I was hooked up with any and all groups that were government watchdogs. I read legislation and told people what the legislation really said. I discussed legislation covering the budget deficit, NAFTA, jobs, immigration, campaign finance reform, election reform, health care, education reform, lobby reform.... I spent most of my time doing the research, helping with meetings, and passing out as much information as possible. I made a point of letting members know how local politicians voted, and what bills they supported, and what it really meant to us.... I started giving lectures outside of UWSA on major issues. I usually had twenty to fifty people attend. I could concentrate on getting information to people and listening to their points without a formal 'meeting' structure. No Robert's Rules!"

Ross Perot speaks

While De was speaking to Ohioans, Ross Perot was speaking to America. During the first six months of 1993, Perot traveled the country appearing at many more rallies than he had during his 1992 presidential campaign. He also made the talk show circuit. He appeared before Congress speaking about government reform, and before a House committee dealing with the North American Free Trade Agreement (NAFTA). Ross Perot was able to buy more infomercial time from NBC, although other networks refused to sell him time for what they called "advocacy ads" (Barta, 1993).

Perot had tapped into the public's anti-status-quo and anti-government feelings. Does this sound familiar? As I write this today, these "feelings" have been proven right, as more business and government corruption is continually exposed. In fact, just recently, at the fitness facility where I train, one of the personal trainers, Gene Bonetti, said to me, "Passing a law is fine, but what about enforcement?" We were discussing illegal immigration, and I first heard his question asked by De Clapsadle in 1993.

De was an "issues" member in UWSA, and there were many others like her. As noted before, there was some turnover among supporters because the emphasis had changed from elections and campaigns to a greater focus on the issues and on educating the people and our government officials. Even with this shift, many of the people who participated in the 1992 presidential campaign also moved into UWSA, recognizing that "The price of freedom is eternal vigilance." For us, that statement from Thomas Jefferson expresses the belief that there are many ways to protect freedom and the Bill of Rights, and that it's up to each one of us. Ross Perot understood that United We Stand America was one of the vehicles that "We the People" could use for that purpose.

Perot and UWSA members and supporters continued to focus on increased citizen involvement in running our country, ethics in government, jobs/NAFTA, and all of the other issues that were raised during Ross Perot's 1992 presidential campaign. However, Perot used new communication methods to get our message across.

Carolyn Barta, in her book *Perot and His People*, discusses the use of the new media. We members of United We Stand America employed direct forms of communication, like town hall meetings with the audience members asking the questions, rather than reporters. We took advantage of call-in shows like *Larry King Live*. Ross Perot pioneered the use of these successful techniques in politics.

Barta said, "The sea change in 1992 was the emergence of 'electronic campaigning' largely exploited by Ross Perot—talk shows, cable TV, electronic town halls, infomercials, campaign videos, satellite television, faxed information, computer bulletin boards—all aimed at a more participatory democracy" (385–87). According to Barta, "In 1982, John Naisbett predicted in his book, *Megatrends*, that America would move away from representative democracy toward a more participatory democracy.... He forecast further that the end of representative democracy would sound the death knell for the two-party system" (p. 387).

The role of the Internet

This growth of a citizen-involved democracy has been aided tremendously by the emergence of the Internet as a source of instantaneous information. The Internet has provided a method of individual and mass communication with people across the country and around the world.

As early as 1992, the Internet—still a primitive medium—became a major means of communication among members and supporters of UWSA. In fact, I was told that in order to be an active participant in United We Stand America I had to learn how to use a computer and e-mail. When my husband and sons first saw me at the computer, they couldn't believe their eyes. I'm not technically or mechanically gifted, to say the least. In fact, even today, if I use a fax or copy machine, I keep my fingers crossed that it's still working afterward.

But, my interest in UWSA gave me a very strong reason to change my ways. If I was going to be active in the growing organization, the Internet needed to be my main method of communication with the members. In fact, even today, we "reformers" still have several active e-mail "reflectors"—address lists for mass e-mailing—providing communication among groups of twenty to one thousand people, where we continue to exchange issue ideas and opinions.

Howard Dean, now the Democratic Party chair, picked up on the Internet and used this vehicle to raise campaign money in 2004 (According to *Plugged-In-Politics*, PBS Online NewsHour, August 5, 2003). But, the main method of communication via the Internet by a political party or movement was pioneered in 1993 by UWSA—the beginning of a communications revolution in politics.

Donna Donovan of Connecticut recalls that in 1992 she became a member of Prodigy, one of the earliest Internet networks, which was so technically basic that it took several days for an e-mail to reach its recipient. On this network, she met Dawn Larson of Illinois and

Jim Callis of Arizona, and the three began to discuss political issues. Later, all three were drawn to the Perot-inspired movement, and all three became activists in their states.

Despite a move toward a more participatory democracy in this country, the other part of Naisbett's prediction—the demise of the two-party system—has yet to occur. Major change in the structure of the United States government and the political system happens at a snail's pace. Our Constitution, with its built-in checks and balances, requires many steps and agreement across many constituencies before change can occur or structural amendments can be added to the United States Constitution.

Once we had more tools like the Internet to inform and communicate with Americans individually, issues seemed to grow in importance. As citizens learned more about the issues and their impact on their own lives, they became more and more inspired to pay closer attention to political news and express their opinions.

Chapter 5

The Mission and Issues of United We Stand America

In 1993 and 1994, the issues that were important to those in UWSA—and to people across America—were the same as those raised by Ross Perot in the 1992 presidential campaign. They included immigration; NAFTA's (the North American Free Trade Agreement) impact on jobs; education reform; health care reform; national debt reduction, including the trade deficit and tax reform; and election reform, including campaign finance reform, term limits, ballot access, negative campaigning, election mechanics, the electoral college, and lobbying reform.

In 1993 and 1994, Newt Gingrich and the Republicans woke up to the American people's interest in the issues focused on by the Perot reform movement and United We Stand America. They adopted them, and incorporated them in their "Contract With America," which contributed to the Republican's success in the congressional elections in 1994 (Gans 1995).

Writing and publishing books on some of these key issues was another communications tool used by Ross Perot. Some of the problems addressed in Ross Perot's books (including *United We Stand; Not For Sale at Any Price; Save Your Job, Save Our Country; Intensive Care; Preparing Our Country for the 21st Century*; and *The Dollar Crisis* coauthored with Senator Paul Simon) are: reducing the budget and trade deficits, improving the United States education system, meeting the health care needs of all citizens from birth to senior citizen status, and reforming the government's campaign finance and lobbying systems. In his books, Ross Perot presented his point of view. His books are clear, charismatic, and understandable—just like the man himself.

The mission

In Ross Perot's 1993 book *Not For Sale at Any Price* (p. 155), he listed many of the goals of United We Stand America:

- To re-create a government that comes from the people—not at the people.
- To reform the federal government at all levels to eliminate waste, fraud, and abuse.
- To have a government where the elected, appointed, and career officials come to serve and not to cash in.
- To get our economy moving and put our people back to work.
- To balance the budget.
- To pay off our nation's debt.
- To build an efficient and cost-effective health care system.
- To get rid of foreign lobbyists.
- To get rid of political action committees.
- To make our neighborhoods and streets safe from crime and violence.
- To create the finest public schools in the world for our children.
- To pass on the American Dream to our children, making whatever fair-shared sacrifices are necessary.

Some of the many reasons people joined United We Stand America were the positions that Ross Perot and the organization took on these and many other issues.

Issues do matter

Some UWSA members wanted to support Ross Perot's stand. Other people joined to represent another point of view, and wanted to convince members to understand and support their position.

Immigration

An example of the variety of views that existed within UWSA became evident when addressing the issue of immigration. The groups of people most interested in this issue in the 1990s were the groups that lived in states where illegal immigrants were beginning to mass: southern states such as North Carolina and southwestern states bordering Mexico—California, Arizona, New Mexico, and Texas. Additionally, any areas where crops needed harvesting or animals needed tending or herding—or Iowa, for instance, where meatpacking plants were plentiful— had people in UWSA who were focused on immigration.

In 1992–94, points of view ranged from an emphasis on tightening border security and preventing illegal immigration, to a temporary halt to any immigration until the problem of massive illegal immigrants crossing the border was resolved. Another group interested in the immigration issue focused on how to address the millions of undocumented immigrants already here.

As indicated in many newspapers and on television newscasts, the estimate of three million illegal immigrants from 2000 has now in 2007 increased to more than twelve million—and perhaps as many as twenty million—because the government, as of the winter 2007, has still failed to fully address the open-border problem. Though not many people understood the potential impact of illegal immigration in 1993–94, today its impact is countrywide, and public interest is very focused and often furious in nature.

Today, public concern about immigration has grown to include the entire country, leading to rallies in many cities and states, telephone calls, e-mails, and letters to members of Congress. This wave of concern even brought Senate business to a halt in April 2006, and in June 2007 created a massive influx of mail and phone calls to Congress and the Senate by those opposing the immigration bill the Senate was attempting to bring to a vote.

This is one example of how the issues addressed by UWSA in 1993 still remain in the public eye today. Partisanship on immigration and other issues has not only increased but hardened. If we had addressed the illegal immigration problem in 1993, we would not have over twelve million undocumented immigrants living in the United States today.

A vast majority of citizens I call "Perot reformers" today believe that in order to solve the illegal immigration problem, both parts of this issue need to be addressed, but in the correct order.

First, the border must be secured. If the illegal immigrants already here are given a path to citizenship before we control the borders, we risk increasing the influx of undocumented workers because we will have created for them a new and easier path to U.S. citizenship. Therefore, we must monitor and fully secure our borders first. The government agency responsible for immigration needs to be reorganized and brought up-to-date technologically. We need a national database to track everyone entering this country. To better control our borders, we need help from citizens, an increase in border patrol members, cameras along the border, support from the National Guard in certain locales, and a fence in the most easily penetrated sections of the border.

Once we have secured our borders, we need to make it very costly for employers to hire undocumented workers. We need to increase fines to a minimum of $50,000 per undocumented immigrant hired, as a loud wake-up call to employers who break the law. And, we need to enforce the immigration laws already passed. These and other steps to reform our immigration laws have been outlined by the Federation of American Immigration Reform (FAIR) and were discussed and debated frequently on CNN's *Lou Dobbs Tonight.*

After we have tightened the borders and addressed the issue of penalizing employers who are breaking the law, we need to evaluate the results of these actions.

This is not an issue that can be solved with one piece of legislation. Congress discovered this fact when the Senate immigration bill was brought to a screeching halt by American citizens letting their representatives know that breaking the law cannot be tolerated, whatever the reason. As Ross Perot has advocated again and again in speeches and interviews, we need to test a little, analyze the results, and then move to the next step.

On the issue of illegal immigration, the reason that the immigration reform bill S.1348 sponsored by Senators Kennedy, Reid, Leahy, Menendez, and Salazar in June 2007 was withdrawn was the direct result of the attention, letters, phone calls, and demonstrations by so many American citizens. As I write this book, we wait and watch to see if existing laws are enforced and if new, fair, and manageable immigration legislation is passed and properly enforced.

The immigration issue is a concrete example of one lesson emphasized in the 1992 Perot presidential campaign, in 1993–95, through the participants in UWSA, and later in the Reform Party. The lesson is clear—the public must get involved for real change to occur. People *can* make a difference when they organize, educate themselves and others, and make their views heard. Today, the immigration problem has produced significant citizen participation on all sides of the issue. However, success by the citizens also requires a committed, well-organized leadership and an organization with a clear direction. The formation of this organization will be discussed in detail in chapter 17.

NAFTA—the North American Free Trade Agreement

The issue of falling wages due to the influx of illegal immigrants coming across the open Mexican border, who are willing to take lower salaries, grew in importance as the numbers increased from three million people before 2000 to over twelve million people in 2007. The North American Free Trade Agreement (NAFTA), signed by President Clinton in 1994, has impacted the United States by encouraging illegal immigration; increasing the trade deficit and the national debt; and reducing the number of well-paid manufacturing jobs in the textile, clothing, car, aircraft, and national defense equipment industries, as the companies move their plants to countries with cheaper labor.

The key NAFTA problem UWSA focused on in the early 1990s was the loss of manufacturing jobs, for which high wages were paid, to countries where salaries were lower. Today, we have seen substantial numbers of high-paying manufacturing jobs leave our country, replaced by lower-paying service jobs. For example, the majority of toy manufacturing has moved from the United States to China. Also, clothing is now mainly produced in far eastern countries like Thailand or China. Robert E. Scott, an economist with the Economic Policy Institute, wrote in a 2003 briefing entitled *The High Price of "Free" Trade: NAFTA's Failure Has Cost the United States Jobs Across the*

Nation, "NAFTA tilted the economic playing field in favor of investors, and against workers and the environment, resulting in a hemispheric 'race to the bottom' in wages and environmental quality."

As Ross Perot pointed out in his 1993 book *Not for Sale at Any Price* (p.135– 36), "We cannot be a superpower or defend ourselves if we are not a major manufacturer." In 1993, Mr. Perot wrote:

- We pay manufacturing workers ten times what they make in Mexico.
- Our companies spend a great deal on health care, retirement, workers' compensation, life insurance, and many other benefits.
- The recently passed [1993] employee-leave bill adds to the cost of manufacturing.
- The minimum wage in the United States was $4.25. The Mexican minimum wage was 58 cents.

According to Ross Perot in *Save Your Job, Save Our Country*, "Ultimately, NAFTA is not a trade agreement but an investment agreement. NAFTA's principal goal is to protect the investment of U.S. companies that build factories in Mexico. This is accomplished by reducing the risk of nationalization, by permitting the return of profits to U.S. businesses, and by allowing unlimited access to the American markets for goods produced in Mexico.

"Does anyone from the United States benefit from NAFTA? Yes, the owners of labor intensive companies that move their factories to Mexico. They can save a minimum of $10,000 for every job they move from the United States to Mexico. In the process, they can avoid U.S. environmental, health, and safety regulations" (11–12).

The vast majority of United We Stand America members agreed with Ross Perot on the NAFTA issue in 1993, and the many United We Stand America veterans I talk to still agree with Ross Perot on this issue today. What's more, the great number of working Americans who have experienced the negative effects of NAFTA on their economic security have been stirred awake as well.

In 1993 and 1994, UWSA volunteers hit the streets, working to convince more Americans to stand up for our jobs and our country by lobbying our elected representatives in Washington not to support or vote for this treaty. Tactics used to get the message out varied from state to state.

In Connecticut in early 1993, the anti-NAFTA drums had started beating loudly. In addition to the 22 percent of state voters who cast their ballots for Perot in 1992, many more were getting the message from Connecticut's own Ralph Nader, who, like Ross Perot, had come out in strong opposition to this trade agreement. Another Connecticut resident, author Martin Gross (whose books exposed the massive impact of government waste) had also joined the anti-NAFTA bandwagon. He was on TV and radio as well as active in speaking in person before audiences around the state. Against this backdrop, the state, which had always had a strong manufacturing base, was beginning to see jobs erode at companies like Stanley Hardware, submarine builder Electric Boat, and aircraft engine maker Pratt & Whitney.

United We Stand America grew quickly in Connecticut, and Donna Donovan recalls that the organizers had been asking Ross Perot to make a personal appearance in their state to help boost the currency of this new organization. "When the number of members who had signed up and paid the $15 membership fee to join UWSA in Connecticut hit twelve thousand people," said Donna, "Perot agreed to make a stop here. We were elated."

Donna remembers, "We aimed high and approached Quinnipiac College [now Quinnipiac University] in Hamden, which gets national media coverage for their political polls, and asked if they'd be willing to host an appearance by Ross. Dr. John Lahey, the school's President, enthusiastically agreed. We chose Sunday, June 13, 1993 as the date, and began letting the press know about the event, which we billed as a rally to build UWSA membership."

"The media ate it up," said Donna. "We got tons of publicity for the rally, but the press engaged in a lot of speculation, too, about Perot's motives for making public appearances. They just couldn't accept that someone they now categorized as a 'politician' was interested in talking to the people for any other reason than to get votes."

Donna had a stack of clippings, and chose one from *The Middletown Press* three days before the rally in which they quoted a political science professor from the University of New Haven commenting about Perot, saying, "He's certainly keeping his political position alive, so that if he decides to run again, he'll be viable."

But the people got it, and they turned out for the rally on a beautiful Sunday afternoon in June. "The crowds started coming hours before the field house doors were even open," remembers Donna. "The mood was really festive. People were wearing patriotic shirts and hats. Some carried signs about NAFTA and other issues as well. One UWSA member, Dick Trainor, of Putnam, who owned a trucking company, brought his POW/MIA semi truck with an amazing tribute to our military printed all over it, and we parked it right in front to attract attention. Ross loved it!"

The field house filled to capacity quickly when the doors opened. Donna recalled, "The school was really prepared, and quickly set up an overflow venue with closed-circuit TV screens for those who couldn't fit in the field house. In the end, we estimated about three thousand people came to see and hear Ross that day—well beyond our wildest dreams.

"Ross received so much applause and standing ovations that I lost count, as he spoke, educating us about government spending, about the growing debt and deficit, and about how passing NAFTA would kill American manufacturing. The mood in that place was supercharged. When Ross talked about taking our country back, the people in that audience really believed they could do it. Ross gave us hope for the future of our country."

In California, according to Judy Duffy from Orange County, the world-famous "Hollywood" sign was changed to "Perotwood" by the strategic placement of bed sheets. Banners were placed above the "Hollywood" sign in the hills, and banners were hung across California freeways. Judy said, "Some people loved [to be part of placing] overpass banners. Some loved [putting up] signs and [participating in] rallies during rush hours. Another woman passed the hat each week to get a plane banner to fly over beaches.... There were button makers, t-shirts, key chains, etc. We did fairs ... for about three years. We did local swap meets most weekends. If we had a hot issue [like NAFTA], flyers, buttons, shirts, etc., we had a crowd. We had local and statewide newsletters and went to the 'Big Mouth,' an automated call-out telephone system. It was time consuming to enter the names, phone numbers, and congressional districts, but as it grew we had great communications without taking phone calls or having to make them."

Many UWSA state organizations would go on to adopt this successful communication system as well.

Mic Farris, in 2006 a thirty-seven-year-old Californian, said, "In 1994, we hosted a rally at the Federal Building in Westwood to bring public awareness to the upcoming vote on NAFTA, receiving network TV coverage for the event."

In New Jersey, Bev Kidder said, "We did a lot of demonstrations against NAFTA. The biggest one was at Allied Signal where we teamed up with the unions and Nader's folks. We held up signs on a four-lane boulevard that said HONK AGAINST NAFTA. There were hundreds of demonstrations and thousands of cars honking.

"Perot, Ralph Nader, Pat Buchanan and Reverend Jesse Jackson had teamed up to oppose NAFTA. ... We had another demonstration with the Nader people outside of New Jersey Congressman Dick Zimmer's office near Trenton.

"Frank Conrad, a wonderful and active volunteer from New Jersey who has since passed away, had arranged for what we called caravans.... Five to a dozen cars would drive up and down the Atlantic City Parkway with American flags flying. They had banners on the sides of the cars that said HONK AGAINST NAFTA, and they had truck drivers blaring their horns, and people in passenger cars honking, and drivers holding their 'thumbs up.' Senior citizens on their way to Atlantic City would slow down to show their support."

In other parts of New Jersey, and in other states as well, these car caravans caught on and many volunteers in anti-NAFTA car caravans drove through small towns all across the state and across America. I personally participated in many of these demonstrations.

In fact, anti-NAFTA views were so strongly held that they produced intense emotional responses. For example, someone threw a book at me during a NAFTA discussion. We even had to lock one member out of a meeting because she lost control and began hitting people who disagreed with her!

In Texas, Paul Truax said, "We did studies on NAFTA and immigration. In our UWSA meetings we had speakers on NAFTA, immigration, the balanced budget and other issues.

"Senator Kay Hutchinson was friendly and listening to UWSA. Congressman Ralph Hall came to many of our meetings and readily returned my phone calls. And we met with Congressman Dick Armey to discuss our issues."

In Michigan, Diane McKelvey was busy with car caravan runs covered with signs reading, "Say NO to NAFTA," "Call Your Congressman," or "Fight Against Job Loss."

Diane said, "We organized a Letters to the Editor writing campaign. I went to the government classes in schools to discuss and explain the negative effects that NAFTA would have on jobs in the United States. Those kids would listen and ask questions. Good questions. My hope was that they would share some of it with their parents. This was a great experience for me.

"When we had our UWSA meetings we would also invite government and Social Studies teachers to bring their classes to attend. We had several meetings where there were more teenagers than volunteers! And they asked good questions too."

Education

As parents, teachers, and students were introduced to United We Stand America through the NAFTA issue, the interest in education began to rise within the organization. Discussion by the members focused on public schools, charter schools, and vouchers.

Ross Perot had been discussing education since the 1980s. In 1987, he said, "Whatever it takes to build the finest education system in the world, we must do. Now that doesn't mean we throw away money. Every penny that goes into education should go squarely into the center of the bull's eye for excellence" (Robinson 1992, 77).

He touched on education and the disadvantaged when he stated in 1986, "The most important thing we can do for people who ... are down on their luck is give them the training and skills. That's the reason I spent a year and a half of my life to reform the Texas schools" (ibid., 79).

In 1992, TV talk show host Phil Donahue noted, "Perot said that if he had only one wish for American schools it would be to get severely disadvantaged children into special schools where they are loved and nurtured, taught how to learn, and are made to feel special by the staff. Perot funds such a school for very young children and it works" (ibid., 80).

Ross Perot said, "We rank at the bottom of the industrialized world in terms of academic achievement, but we are spending $328 billion a year on public education systems" (ibid., 76).

In fact, many wealthy parents, parents of disadvantaged students, and parents of gifted children wanted their taxes used to fund private schools that provide a more disciplined and demanding education. They wanted the government to issue vouchers to be used in these private education facilities. The amount of the voucher would be based on how much per child their public school received in public funding. Many members of UWSA supported the voucher program.

Other UWSA participants favored the formation of charter schools that were also funded with public school monies. However, charter schools were not private and fell under the jurisdiction of a town or city school board. These schools were usually organized around a particular method of education, such as team teaching, or centered on a special curriculum, such as the arts or sciences.

Some UWSA participants still supported public schools and believed these alternative means of educating our students removed money and reduced improvements to our public school system.

There was one point upon which all UWSA members agreed: everyone needs to get involved in the education of the community's children—school administrators, teachers, parents, elected officials, business leaders, and local residents.

The education issue was an example of the differing views and exchange of ideas that United We Stand America encompassed. The emphasis on and thoughtful discussion of education also demonstrated the importance of this issue to American citizens, the majority of whom continue to believe today that education still has not been successfully addressed in most areas of the United States. In fact, *Tough Choices or Tough Times*, a major report published in early 2007 by the National Center on Education and the Economy, concluded that the American education system is not keeping up with other countries, and that, "A major overhaul is needed, and while it may seem dramatic, the very future of our country depends on it" (U.S. education needs sweeping reform, *Denver Post*, February 3, 2007).

Health care reform

Health care, like education, has been (and still is) in crisis in the United States. From my personal experiences with the health care system and the opinions of the thousands of people I have spoken to about this topic, I believe the crisis has been precipitated by the following factors:

- Growing cost of medical care
- Lack of health insurance coverage for forty-seven million Americans
- Creation of HMOs (health maintenance organizations) that increase the role of insurance companies in health care decisions, while reducing the role of doctors and patients
- Increasing cost of Medicare and Medicaid as baby boomers age
- Increased complexity of insurance and government rules and regulations to the point where an advanced college degree is almost required to interpret and comply
- Growth of the medical bureaucracy in hospitals that leads to medical errors and soaring costs

In 1994, the major health care issue was the increasing costs of Medicare and Medicaid. In Ross Perot's book *Intensive Care*, he clearly states, "People do not want the government telling them what kind of health care they can and cannot have. What is needed is reform of the health care financing system that would not jeopardize the quality of health care" (39).

This statement was spot-on then and remains so today. The health care financing system is still broken. In fact, with the introduction of HMOs, insurers restrict the patients' choice of doctors to those only approved by the HMO. If patients choose doctors outside of the list, many insurers will not cover the cost. In addition, if a medial treatment is not on the HMO list of approved procedures, the insurer will again not pay for the treatment. In fact, a November 2006 poll indicates that, regardless of age or political affiliation, more Americans see the need for health care reform as the top problem facing the nation today, with the exception of the war in Iraq (Newport 2007).

In fact, in 1991, Donna Donovan and her husband, Ken Thornley—who passed away in 2006—experienced their own personal version of the national health care crisis when Ken was diagnosed with a rare sinus cavity cancer. The year before, he had lost his job in publishing after twenty-three years—and along with that his health insurance. Donna, who is self-employed, then added him to her policy, which she bought through a group for the self-employed. "I thought we were okay," said Donna, "but I never imagined what we were in for." Ken had surgery, underwent radiation treatments, and eventually was declared cancer free.

Donna explained what happened during the next few years. "We learned what it means to be 'under-insured.' Our premiums climbed from $230 per month to more than $1,200 per month. When added to out-of-pocket expenses not covered by insurance, we were eventually spending about twenty-five percent of our income for health care! And I lived in fear of anything happening to me because I was working 60 to 80 hours most weeks just trying to keep us afloat."

After two rejected applications over as many years, Ken eventually qualified for Social Security disability. This made him eligible for Medicare, taking some of the pressure off and allowing Donna to shop for insurance for herself alone. Though Ken's cancer never recurred, he suffered several strokes from 2003 to 2006, when he passed away. Due to his cancer—considered by insurance companies as a preexisting condition—Ken was never able to qualify for long-term care insurance. His final illness and disability ran up substantial homecare and nursing home debts that Medicare and the Medigap supplemental plan they had purchased from an insurance company didn't cover.

Of the experience she and her husband went through, Donna said, "When it comes to your financial security, all it takes is one medical crisis and no matter how well you think you're protected, all you can do is stand there and watch it fall apart. Our health care system is sick at its core, and Band-Aid solutions just won't fix it."

Like Donna, I have had to depend on the health care system more and more since 1993 and I have come to believe that anyone extensively involved with today's medical system needs an advocate. You need a friend or a family member who can attend all sessions with the doctor as a backup listener, and someone who closely tracks your medication and care at a hospital and at your home. Watching the cost and billing for overcharges and double charges for the same procedure is required. I have found both medical and billing errors to be common in today's medical arena.

While billing errors are troubling enough, the medical negligence and errors are downright frightening. In fact, I recently was rushed to a hospital emergency room with a heart rate of 29. The cause of this problem was overmedication. Two years ago, I had a heart condition that required medication to slow down my heart rate and keep my blood pressure low. However, the condition cleared up, and the doctor continued to keep me on that medication. When I caught a stomach virus, the medication (which I no longer needed) caused a major drop in my heart rate, which could have been fatal. I was rushed to the hospital and placed in intensive care. The problem medication was stopped, and I miraculously improved.

Many UWSA members were concerned about the health care issue in the 1990s. Nothing has happened since to ease their concern—quite the opposite.

Debt, deficits, and tax reform

Health care is certainly not the only area of American life in which rising costs need to be addressed. Our national debt has more than doubled between 2000 and 2007 to $8.83 trillion, and Washington has passed three tax cuts (in 2001, 2003, and 2006) which have had the effect of reducing revenues and expanding the budget deficit (Heritage Foundation backgrounder #2001, January 27, 2007). Remember, it's not just the debt, but also the interest on that debt, which now equals over $2,000 per person per year. The national debt is like a home mortgage where the interest paid over fifteen, twenty, or thirty years can be many times more than the actual debt itself. We need to reduce our yearly deficit to reduce the overall long-term debt. Perot explains this clearly in his book *Not for Sale at Any Price* when he states, "The deficit is one year's increase in the [overall national] debt.... During the years when we take in more money than we spend, a budget surplus [instead of a deficit] occurs and the debt is paid down" (26–28).

In the 1990s, our elected representatives attempted to reduce the national debt by running yearly budget surpluses. From 1997 during the Clinton administration through 2000 when George W. Bush was elected, they did achieve a budget surplus (Source: United States Office of Management and Budget), although it failed to greatly slow the growth of the national debt. And since the Bush administration took office, the budget and the debt have soared.

In fact, since George W. Bush became president, when the national debt stood at $5.6 trillion, our debt has continued to rise. As I write this book, the debt is rapidly approaching the debt limit set by Congress just last year at $9 trillion, which will soon put Congress in the position of having to authorize more debt (*NPR Morning Edition*, "Congress Sets New Federal Debt Limit," March 16, 2006).

What about our country's trade deficit? A trade deficit occurs when American consumers buy more products from other countries than we sell to other countries. It's more bad news. The U.S. trade deficit has continued to rise every year without interruption since 1973 (Source: Federal government office of the U.S. Census Bureau, Foreign Trade Division).

Consider, too, our balance of trade with individual countries. First, consider Mexico. Prior to the passage of NAFTA in January 1994, our balance of trade with that country fluctuated near zero—between surplus and deficit. Since 1994, as virtually all restrictions on trade and investment between our countries have been phased out, our trade deficit with Mexico has been steadily rising, exceeding $64 billion in 2006 (Sources: Congressional Budget Office; U.S. Census Bureau, Foreign Trade Division).

And what about China? In 1985, U.S. trade with China already put us in the deficit column to the tune of approximately $6 million. As of 2006, our deficit had surpassed $232 trillion! (Source: U.S. Census Bureau, Foreign Trade Division)

If it seems that our country is headed in the wrong direction not just with our trade deficit but also with the national debt and deficit, it's because we are—at record-breaking speed. We can concede that some of the recent increase is due to the war in Iraq and the war on terrorism. Legislated tax cuts have also contributed to the rise in the annual deficit and the long-term national debt. But where will it end? Where are the politicians with the drive and the plan to put our country back in the plus column? I'm still looking. Keep in mind, also, that rising Social Security, Medicare, and Medicaid costs will continue to increase as the baby boomers generation moves into its senior years. As Ross Perot put it, "No one in Washington tells you that we can't keep running up these deficits and that the debt is destroying our country and our children's future" (1993, 28).

Part of the solution to the out-of-control deficit and debt is to address real tax reform. Over the years, our tax system has become extremely complex as our government layers an ever-deepening and growing patchwork of small changes over the tax code, without looking at the total picture. It's like accumulating furniture, paper, and junk in your basement until you can't even go down the stairs anymore. Cleanup was way overdue in 1992, and it's reached critical mass today. Now is the time to clean out the basement.

In order to successfully address the reforms critical to our national fiscal system, we need to focus on the people elected to make these changes, as well as the system that puts those people into office.

Election reform

Before any of the other problems facing our country can be effectively addressed and reformed, we need to elect people who will listen to us, the citizens of this country—elected officials who will truly represent our interests and will pledge to make the necessary changes. But, in order to get people like this elected, we've got to fix our terribly broken election system at the national, state, and local levels.

Included in this broad category of election reform are the following issues:

- Campaign finance reform
- Term limits
- Voting day
- Election mechanics
- Negative campaigning
- The electoral college
- Lobbying
- Ballot access

The issue of campaign finance reform (CFR) received the most attention in UWSA and from the federal government from 1993 to 1995.

To begin with, the people need to understand the legal basis on which the campaign finance issue is framed. The next section, "Buckley v. Valeo"—which was written and sent to campaign finance reform UWSA state leaders in 1995 by Michael Dunn, the UWSA California CFR task force cochairman—laid the groundwork for this understanding.

Buckley v. Valeo

On January 30, 1976, the Supreme Court handed down an opinion in Buckley v. Valeo that rewrote the rule book for congressional and presidential campaign fundraising and spending, creating a legal paradigm for reform that stands untouched 17 years later.

The Supreme Court's multifaceted decision set the precedents on a host of issues. The court ruled that it was unconstitutional to impose mandatory spending limits on campaigns, to prohibit unlimited personal spending by candidates on their own behalf or to prohibit independent campaigns for or against candidates.

At the same time, the court sanctioned voluntary spending limits as a condition for receiving public funding. It also approved disclosure requirements for campaign spending and receipts and limits on contributions from individuals and political committees.

Contribution Limits

By a 6–2 vote, the court upheld limits on campaign contributions. Under the statute, which is unchanged, individuals may give $1000 to a candidate for each election, with an overall contribution limit of $25,000 a year. Political Action Committees [PACs] may give $5000 to a candidate for each election, with no annual aggregate limit.

The court found that the contribution caps do not significantly undermine an individual's First Amendment right of freedom of speech.

"A limitation upon the amount that any one person or group may contribute to a candidate or political committee entails only a marginal restriction upon the contributor's ability to engage in free communication," the majority said. The limits permit "symbolic expression of support evidenced by a contribution" but do not "infringe the contributor's freedom to discuss candidates and issues."

The court found no evidence that the contribution caps discriminated against challengers, minor party candidates or independents.

Contribution and Spending Disclosures

The court sustained the law's public disclosure provisions on a 7–1 vote, with Burger dissenting. The law required campaigns to disclose contributions of $100 or more and expenditures of more than $10. (In 1979, the law was changed to require disclosure of aggregate contributions and expenditures of $200 or more).

The justices found "no constitutional infirmities in the record-keeping, reporting and disclosure provisions" but cautioned that they should be treated carefully so as not to harm minor party candidates and members.

To exempt themselves from disclosures, minor party candidates "need only show a reasonable probability that the compelled disclosure of a party's contributors' names will subject them to threats, harassment or reprisals from either government officials or private parties."

In his dissent, Burger wrote that the levels at which the disclosure were required were "irrationally low."

Public Financing

The court held 6–2 that Congress had the power to provide public financing for presidential elections and national party conventions.

The justices found that the use of public money to subsidize candidates did not favor established parties over new parties or incumbents over challengers. Major party candidates receive full funding for the general election and matching funds during the primary; minor parties do not receive any funds in their first campaign unless they win more than 5% of the vote in the general election, in which case federal funds can be used to help retire the debt. They would then be entitled to full funding the next time out.

The formula, the court wrote, "is a congressional effort, not to abridge, restrict or censor speech but rather to use public money to facilitate and enlarge public discussion and participation in the electoral process, goals vital to a self-governing people ... The inability, if any, of minority party candidates to wage effective campaigns will derive not from lack of public financing but from their inability to raise private contributions."

In a footnote, the court said the conditions established for acceptance of public funds—including otherwise unconstitutional spending limits—were permissible. In a subsequent case designed to draw the court out on this point, Republican National Committee v. Federal Election Commission, the court in 1979 refused to reconsider a lower court ruling that the presidential system was constitutional.

Spending Limits

The court ruled 7–1 that imposition of mandatory spending limits is an unconstitutional abridgement of a candidate's First Amendment rights. The court reasoned that spending caps impinge on a candidate's ability to communicate freely and forcefully to voters.

"This is because virtually every means of communicating ideas in today's mass society requires the expenditure of money," the court wrote. "The electorate's increasing dependence on television, radio and other mass media for news and information has made these expensive modes of communication indispensable instruments of effective speech.

"The expenditure limitations contained in the Act represent substantial rather than merely theoretical restraints on the quantity and diversity of political speech."

The court did acknowledge that contribution limits, like spending limits, have First Amendment implications, but distinguished between the two by saying that the law's "expenditure ceilings impose significantly more severe restrictions on protected freedom of political expression and association than do its limitations on financial contributions."

Independent Expenditures

Without dissent, the court struck a provision that would have capped spending by independent campaigns for or against a candidate at $1300. It said the provision was a clear violation of the First Amendment.

"While the (independent spending ceiling) fails to serve any substantial government interest in stemming the reality or appearance of corruption in the electoral process, it heavily burdens core First Amendment expression," the court wrote.

"Advocacy of the election or defeat of candidates for federal office is no less entitled to protection under the First Amendment than the discussion of political policy generally or advocacy of the passage or defeat of legislation."

Personal Spending

The court also ruled 6–2 that the limit on spending by a candidate on his or her own behalf was unconstitutional. The law had set a $25,000 limit on House candidates, $35,000 on Senate candidates and $50,000 on presidential candidates.

"The candidate, no less than any other person, has a First Amendment right to engage in the discussion of public issues and vigorously and tirelessly to advocate his own election and the election of other candidates," the opinion said.

In the ruling, the court dismissed concerns that unlimited personal spending enabled candidates to avoid the impact of the contribution limits. In essence, it said that a candidate can not corrupt him or herself.

"The use of personal funds reduces the candidate's dependence on outside contributions and thereby counteracts the coercive pressures and attendant risks of abuse to which the Act's contribution limitations are directed," wrote the majority.

Once we in New Jersey understood the legal underpinnings of the CFR issue presented above by Michael Dunn, we decided to directly address the need for reform. In 1994, six members of UWSA New Jersey decided to study the campaign contributions made in the 1993 New Jersey state election for governor. The six members included: Larry Pelosi, CFR Project Manager; Rosemarie Deal, CFR Project Analyst; Milton Benjamin, Computer Systems Analyst; Al Gautier, Software Database Analyst; Ray Rhoads, Project Analyst for a local study (Gloucester Township) and application of our newly created software database; and I served as CFR team leader. In addition, forty UWSANJ volunteers supported us working on data entry.

In New Jersey's capitol of Trenton, we waded through eighteen thousand pages of CFR reports. At the same time, we were creating a database to accept this information so that we could show where contributions came from and to whom these contributions went. Our thinking was that this data could then be used to demonstrate a possible link between our elected state officials and those who provided the money for their election.

At the state level of government, we identified the fifteen major contributors. This list included six PACs, as well as trial lawyers, building contractors, and contributors in the medical, real estate, and business trade categories. Other contributors included a pharmaceutical company and a cigarette manufacturer.

We identified fourteen categories of people who provided 90 percent of the cash funds contributed during this campaign. The results are in figures 5.1 and 5.2 that follow.

UNITED WE STAND AMERICA
New Jersey Office
100 Metroplex Drive - Suite 202
Edison, New Jersey 08817
Tel: (800) 964-7677
Fax: (908) 985-0704

CAMPAIGN FINANCE REFORM (CFR) - DATABASE

1993 Campaign -- Contributions Made to Winning Candidates for the State Legislature

The following list contains the 14 categories of people who contributed 93% of the cash funds collected during this campaign:

1)   Political Parties (30% of total)

2)   Building Sector and Industrials (15% of total)

3)   Medical Industry (11% of total)

4)   Attorneys (9% of total)

5)   Other Professionals, including 'Consultants and nonprofit Groups (7% of total)

6)   Labor Organizations (5% of total)

7)   Financial and Insurance (4% of total)

8)   Food-, Beverages, and Hotels (3% of total)

9)   Automotive and Transportation (3% of total)

10)   Accountants (2% of total)

11)   Individuals (2% of total)

12)   Utilities and Fuel, Industry (2% of total)

13)   Education (1% of total)

14)   Tobacco Industry (1% of total)

**Percentages were rounded off

Page 1 New Jersey Campaign Finance Contributions Breakout

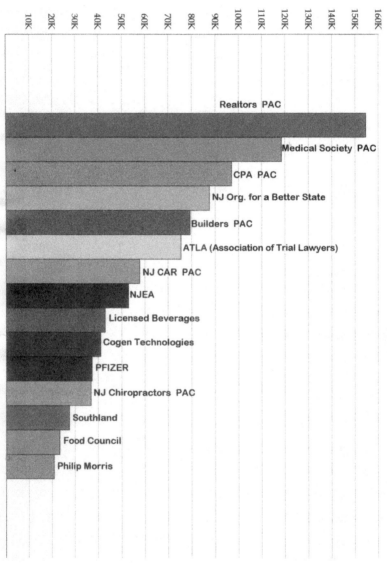

10K 20K 30K 40K 50K 60K 70K 80K 90K 100K 110K 120K 130K 140K 150K 160K

15 LARGEST CASH CONTRIBUTORS

Realtors PAC

Medical Society PAC

CPA PAC

NJ Org. for a Better State

Builders PAC

ATLA (Association of Trial Lawyers)

NJ CAR PAC

NJEA

Licensed Beverages

Cogen Technologies

PFIZER

NJ Chiropractors PAC

Southland

Food Council

Philip Morris

Page 1 Campaign cash contribution Bar Graph

At the local level, we analyzed the 1994 municipal election in one township, hoping to demonstrate with this data the direct link between local election contributions and awarded contracts. Some of what we found was detailed in a newspaper editorial about our study: "*[Fifty-four] percent of contributions to the winning campaign came from people or firms with a direct financial interest in the outcome.* [Emphasis mine.] Eighty-one percent of campaign contributions came from nonresidents.... Pat Benjamin of Cherry Hill who led the team, identified the main trouble areas: lax campaign law enforcement and too much money from political action committees, out-of-state donors and party organizations. Benjamin thinks only contributions from constituents should be allowed.... It is through organizational efforts like this that true reform comes about" (*Courier-Post*. Cherry Hill, New Jersey. Editorial. September 18, 1995).

The state and local studies were completed and presented to the media on September 13, 1995. Numerous newspapers throughout New Jersey picked up the information.

The material contained in our study—the Gloucester Township Report follows.

UWSA - NJ

Project Reform

Report
1994 Municipal Election in

Gloucester Township
Camden County

First Page UWSA Project Reform Report

Introduction

In January 1994, UNITED WE STAND AMERICA-NEW JERSEY, adopted as one of its major state issues Campaign Finance Reform. As part -of our effort It was necessary for our membership and the public at large to be aware of who contributed to election campaigns and what influence they had on our elected officials.

Our first step in this process was to copy over 18,000 pages of reports filed with New Jersey Election Law Enforcement Commission, known as NJ ELEC, by the elected candidates 'for the State Senate and State Assembly in November 1993.

After reviewing these reports by legislative district each contribution of $200.00 or more was classified, by members of UWSA - NJ, into five categories as follows:

Constituent of elected official
Democratic Party controlled PAC's
Republican Party controlled PAC's
Industry and Special Interest PAC's
Businesses and Non-Constituent Individuals

Each of the above categories was broken down into 99 specific areas by use of a two digit code to identify the contributor. (That is, Accountant, Lobbyist, News Media, etc.) Upon completion of the coding all information was entered into a computer database. The information that is generated by this database will be made available to members of UWSA -NJ and the general public so they will be informed voters on election day.

As this project has progressed members of UWSA - NJ have, following the above procedures, gathered, classified and computerized similar information for other local and federal offices.

The information that has been gathered has led to many questions being raised about how to control the influence campaign contributions have on our elected officials. **It is our hope that real Campaign Finance Reform will be the end result of the effort put forth by the many volunteer's who made this database possible.**

Second Page UWSA Project Reform Report

PROJECT REFORM

GLOUCESTER TOWNSHIP
Camden County

General

The following information is an effort to show the voters of Gloucester Township, how the 1994 municipal election campaign was financed. We will show who contributed, how much each contributed and what if any connection the contributor has with the government of Gloucester Township.

The **information contained herein was** obtained by United We Stand America - New Jersey from campaign finance reports filed by the candidates campaign committees with NJ Election Law Enforcement Commission and from public records of Gloucester Township.

It is not our intention to comment on the merits of the arguments for or against either side in this election.

The Election

The Municipal Election of 1994 was held on May 10, between two slates of candidates for the office of Mayor and three seats on town council.

The slates were:

The Incumbents: Gloucester twp Campaign 94

Mayor -- Sandra L. Love

Council -- Helen M. Albright
George H. Genzel, Sr.
Samuel M. Siler

The Challengers: A New Team For Change

Mayor -- Stephen A. Iatarola

Council -- David Ragonese
Arthur F Knapp III
Carol Fabietti

Of the 25,213 registered voters in Gloucester Township only 7,090 voted on election day. The results were:

For Mayor
Incumbents   4,649
Challengers   2,368

For Council
Incumbents ....   4,591 Avg.
Challengers ....   2,349 Avg.

In all races the incumbents were the winners therefore we will focus our attention on them. (Appendix A contains a complete listing of the contributors.)

Third Page UWSA Project Reform Report

Gloucester Twp. Citizens for Responsible Government

Recd from Elect. Fund of	
Ann A. Mullen	($3,150.69)
Other Contributions	$1,700.00
Total Contribution.........	$1,700.00

Note: This is an ongoing political committee that operates through out the year. We have only included transactions as they relate to the candidates in this election.

Gloucester Twp. Campaign 94'

Good Government Team	$ 801.70
Campaign Exp. Reimbursement from Elect. Fund of Sandra Love	($ 5,319.48)
Recd from Gloucester Twp. Citizens for Responsible Gov't. (in Kind)	($ 1,275.00)
Recd from Gloucester Twp. Citizens for Responsible Gov't	$ 365.70
Other Contributions	$33,900.00
Total Contributions	$35,067.40

Following The Money

In Following The Money we will show who contributed the money to finance the campaign of the incumbents. For the purpose of this study we have eliminated the money the candidates used from prior elections as it is not possible to accurately determine the source of these funds.

The first breakdown shows the difference between the contributions from residents of Gloucester Twp. (The Voters) and non residents. Included in the non -resident totals are contributions from companies and PAC's who of course are not eligible to vote in any election.

Residents – 10%

Non Residents – 81%

Not Reportable – 9%

This breakdown shows the contributors classified by business affiliation. The grouping for this breakdown is as follows:

Engineers & Engineering Firms --	$18,000.00
Attorneys --	$10,000.00
Building Industry –	Almost $11,000.00
Financial Industry –	Just under $3000.00
Contributions not reportable by contributor --	$5000.00
Miscellaneous –	Almost $7000

Fourth Page UWSA Project Reform Report

Financing The Campaign

In the election of 1994 the incumbents were well financed, receiving over $65,000.00 in contributions, outspending their opponents by more than 3 to 1.

In addition they set up an elaborate web of committees that received contdbutions from many sources. The chart at the bottom of the page shows these committee's and the direction the money flowed between the committee's. The following is an income summary of each of those committee's.

Election Fund of Friends of Helen M. Albright

Transfer from prev. campaign	$1,185.00
Other contributions	$1,445.00
Total Income	$2,630.00

Election Fund of Ann Mullen

Transfer from Friends of Ann Mullen	$8,973.33
Recd from Elect. Fund of Sandra Love	$3,561.91
Other contributions	$246.57
Total Income	$12,781.81

Election Fund of Sandra Love

Recd from Elect. Fund of Ann Mullen	($ 1,500.00)
Recd from Gloucester Twp. Citizens for Responsible Gov't	($ 425.00)
Recd from Gloucester Twp. Citizens for Responsible Gov't	$121.90
Other contributions	$13,450.00
Total Income	$13,571.90

Fifth Page UWSA Project Reform Report

As you can see Engineers were the leading contributors to the incumbents campaign. They were followed by Attorney's and the Building Industry.

In reviewing these results it should be noted that Professional Service Contracts are awarded by Gloucester Twp., The MUA and the two School Districts without benefit of competitive bidding.

Since Engineers, Attorneys and Architects are the largest recipient of these contracts it could explain the results of this study.

The next breakdown shows what if any monetary interest a contributor might have in making a contribution to the incumbent candidates.

To do this we classified the contributors into five categories as follows:

1. Contributors with a monetary interest. **(54%)**

2. Contributions from previous campaigns of candidates and other Continuing Political Committees. **(16%)**

3. Contributions with no known ties to Gloucester Township Government. **(15%)**

4. Contributions not reportable by contributor. (Contributions of under $200.00) **(8%)**

5. Contributions from Developers, Building Managers, Real Estate interests, etc. **(7%)**

With just over 54% of the total contributions those with a financial interest in the outcome of the election were by far the largest contributors to the incumbents.

These contributors include Engineers, Attorneys, Accountants and Contractors who in 1994 received fees and contracts totaling more than $ 2.7 million in taxpayer dollars.

Although the smallest in terms of percentage,7%, another group that has a financial interest would be the Developers, Building Managers and Real Estate firms. All are either regulated by or must have approval of the Township Planning Board, Zoning Board etc. to conduct their business in Gloucester Township.

The list that follows shows the contributors employer, the amount of the contribution and the amount of taxpayers dollars received by that individual or their employer.

Sixth Page UWSA Project Reform Report

CONTRIBUTORS RECEIVING FINANCIAL COMPENSATION FROM GLOUCESTER TOWNSHIP

Company	Total Contribution's	Position	Compensation
Richard A. Alaimo Assoc. of Engineers	$2,500.00	Engineer	Recd more than $399,000.00 in Professional Service Fees from Glou. Twp. between 1992 and 1994
Blank, Rome Comisky McCauley	$1,000.00	Glou. Twp- Bond Counsel	Recd $35,608.00 in Professional Service Fees from Gloucester Twp. in 1994
David F.Carlamere	$ 500.00	Twp. Solicitor	Receives a salary of between $40,000.00 and $43,050.00 from Gloucester Twp. Exact amount unavailable.
Janet Cokas	$ 500.00	Secretary Glou. Twp. MUA	Salary Unavailable.
Patrick Cokas	$500.00	Personnel Glou. Twp. MUA	Salary Unavailable.
Consulting Engineer Services	$ 2,500.00	Glou. Twp. MUA Engineer	Recd $ 202,124.40 in Professional Service Fees from The Gloucester Twp. MUA in 1994
C. DeSorte Assoc.	$250.00	Paving Contractor	Reed $ 902,963.00 in paving contracts from Gloucester Twp. in FY 1994
Drews & Lowe, Inc.	$500.00	Engineer's	Recd. $35,010.00 in Professional Service Fees in 1994 from Gloucester Twp.
Dun - Rite Sand & Gravel Co.	$ 1,000.00	Building Materials	Recd $ 6,238.53 from Gloucester Twp. for purchases in FY 1994.
Higgins, Slachetka & Long	$2,000.00	Twp. Attorney	Recd $ 78,298.00 in Professional Service Fees from Gloucester Twp. in 1994. Over the three year period 1992 through 1994 Reed $439,484.00.
Kearney & Brady, PC	$750.00	Zoning Board Solicitor	Recd $ 8,465.00 in Professional Service Fees from Gloucester Twp. in 1994.
Key Engineers	$1,000.00	Engineers	Recd $ 72,436.00 in Professional Service Fees from Gloucester Twp. in 1994.

Seventh Page UWSA Project Reform Report

Company	Contribution's		Position Compensation
Joseph Lafferty & Sons, Inc.	$ 750.00	Contractor	Recd $ 243,927.00 from Gloucester Twp. FY 1994 for contracts which they were awarded.
Maressa Goldstein Birsner Patterson Drinkwater & Oddo	$1,500.00	Glou. Twp. MUA Solicitor	Recd. $ 25,077.02 in Professional Service Fees from Gloucester Twp. MUA in 1994.
Michael J. McKenna, Esq.	**$2,000.00**	Planning Board Solicitor	Recd $ 26,294.00 in Professional Service Fees from Gloucester Twp.in 1994.
Paschon & Feurey	$ 500.00	Glou. Twp. Attorney for Gems Landfill	Recd. $13,152.00 from Gloucester Twp. in Professional Service Fees during 1994.
PRD Management, Inc,	$ 500.00	Real Estate Mgt. Co.	Recd. $ 77,708.03 from Gloucester Twp. in Community Development Block Grant Funds in FY 1994.
Remington & Vernick Engineers	$7,700.00	Twp. Engineer	Recd $559,232.00 in Professional Service Fees from Gloucester Twp. in 1994.
Thomas J. Scangarello Associates	$ 500.00	Twp. Planner	Recd $97,290.00 in Professional Service Fees from Gloucester Twp in 1994
Frank C. Schmitt, R.M.A.	$1,500.00	Twp. Auditor	Recd $89,444.00 in Professional Service Fees from Gloucester Twp. in 1994.
Gerald A. Sinclair	$ 750.00	Glou. Twp. Attorney for Capital Projects and Rent Board Solicitor	Recd $ 14,756.00 in Professional Service Fees from Gloucester Twp. in 1994 and $ 83,000.00 Between 1992 & 1994
The Tarquini Organization	$1,000.00	Architect	Has received $101,402.25 in Professional Service Fees from Black Horse Pike Reg. School Dist.from July1,1994 through April,
1995			
John D. Wade, Esq.	$1,000.00	Housing Authority Solicitor, Attorney for Glou. Twp. and Black Horse Pike Reg. School Dist	Recd. a total of $ 140,612.25 in 1994 from Gloucester Twp School Dist ...and Black Horse Pike Reg. School Dist..in Professional
United Computer Sales & Services	$1,000.00	Computer Sales	Recd $113,864.00 in payments on a non bid contract from Gloucester Twp in FY 1994 for new computers.

Eighth Page UWSA Project Reform Report

Appendix A
Incumbent Contributors

Contributor	Employer	Total Amount	Resident	Catagory
Richard Alaimo	Richard A. Alaimo Assoc. of Enges.	$ 2,500.00	Non-Res.	Engineers
Herbert Barness	Herbert Barness, Inc.	$ 250.00	Non-Res.	Builder - Developer
Anthony Bentivegna	Today's Haircutting	$ 250.00	Resident	
Peter Boyer	Blank, Rome, Comisky & McCauley $	500.00	Non-Res,	Attorney's
Dr. John Buzzi	Kupper Associates	$ 500.00	Non- Res	Engineers
Anthony Calabrese	United Computer Sales & Service	$ 1,000.00	Resident	Computer Sales
James Calangelo	Consulting Engineer Services	$ 2,500.00	Non-Res.	Engineers
David Carlamere	David Carlamere	$ 500.00	Resident	Attorney
Janet Cokas	Gloucester Twp. MUA	$ 500.00	Resident	MUA Employee
Patrick Cokas	Gloucester Twp. MUA	$ 500.00	Resident	MUA Employee
Anthony Costa	Anthoney P. Costa	$ 250.00	Non-Res	Attorney
Charles De Sorte	C. De Sorte Assoc.	$ 250.00	Non-Res	Contractor
Richard Drews	Drews & Lowe Inc.	$ 500.00	Non-Res	Engineers
Dun - Rite Sand & Gravel Co.		$ 500.00	N/A	Developer
Charles Dutill	Heritage Technical Services, Inc.	$ 750.00	Non-Res.	Engineers
Election Fund of Ann Mullen		$ 4,650.69	N/A	Political Committee
Election Fund of Sandra Love		$ 3,561.91	N/A	Political Committee
John Federico	Jefferson Repo	$ 750.00	Non-Res.	
Bill & Sharon Finlayson	The Bleznak Organization	$ 500.00	Non-Res.	Real Estate
William Finlayson III	The Bleznak Organization	$ 500.00	Non-Res.	Real Estate
Peter Galetto	Dun - Rite Sand & Gravel Co.	$ 500.00	Non-Res.	Developer

Ninth Page UWSA Project Reform Report

Contributor	Employer	Amount	Resident	Catagory
Good Government Team		$ 801.07	N/A	Political Committee
Thomas Higgins	Higgins, Slachetka & Long	$ 1,000.00	Non-Res.	Attorney
K. Hovnanian @ Valleybrook		$ 500.00	N/A	Developer
IBEW Local 439		$ 250.00	N/A	Labor Union
Lou Joyce	Lou Joyce 3RD,	$ 500.00	Resident	Real Estate
John Kearney	Kearney& Brady, PC	$ 750.00	Non-Res	Attorney
Joseph Lafferty	Joseph Lafferty & Sons, Inc	$ 250.00	Non-Res.	Contractor
Joseph Lafferty & Sons, Inc.		$ 500.00	N/A	Contractor
Joseph Lisiewski	Lisiewski - Murphy	$ 1,000.00	Non- Res	Project Managers
Howard Long, Jr.	Higgins, Slachetka & Long	$ 500.00	Non-Res	Attorney
Robert Lord		$ 1,000.00	Non-Res	
Joseph Maressa	Maressa Goldstein Birsner Patterson Drinkwater & Oddo	$ 1,500.00	Non-Res	Attorney
James Mc Grath	PRD Management, Inc	$ 500.00	Non-Res	Building Mgt,
Michael Mc Kenna	Michael J. McKenna Esq.	$ 2,000.00	Non-Res.	Attorney
Operating Engineers Local 825		$ 300.00	N/A	Labor Union
Robert Paschon	Paschon & Feurey	$ 500.00	Non- Res	Attorney
Kevin Piccolo	Ray Piccolo, Inc.	$ 750.00	Resident	Real Estate
Ray Piccolo	Ray Piccolo, Inc.	$ 250.00	Resident	Real Estate
Richard Piccolo	Pennoni Associates	$ 250.00	Resident	Engineer's
Craig Remington	Remington & Vernick Engineers	$ 6,000.00	Non-Res	Engineer's
Remington & Vernick Engineers		$ 1,700.00	N/A	Engineer's
Charles Riebel	Key Engineers	$ 1,000.00	Non-Res	Engineer's
Thomas Scangarello	Thomas J. Scangarello & Assoc.	$ 500.00	Non-Res	Town Planner

Tenth Page UWSA Project Reform Report

At the same time New Jersey and other states were focusing on campaign finance reform at the state level, members of Congress were working on CFR legislation. United We Stand America members from across the country were working with their federal representatives. Two people from Congress with whom I personally interacted on this issue during the 1990s were Congressman Bob Franks, representing the seventh district in New Jersey; and Congresswoman Linda Smith, from the third district in the state of Washington. In fact, Linda Smith had been elected to Congress as a write-in candidate because she had a stated interest in campaign finance reform. However, neither member of Congress was able to get any CFR legislation passed. Then, after 2000, the CFR legislation sponsored by Senator John McCain passed into law, but only touched on one section of this extensive issue.

Why would any incumbent elected official at any level of government change the campaign finance laws that helped him or her get elected in the first place?

One way to start moving toward meaningful campaign finance reform is to limit the length of time an elected official can serve in the office to which he or she is elected. Imposition of term limits on those voted into office encourages people to provide a public service to their country and then return to the private sector. People voted in under term limits are more likely to truly represent the citizens of this country because they won't be representatives for too long. They won't be able to become "career politicians," a state which was never intended by our founding fathers, who assumed that limited terms would be served by "citizen legislators," who would then return to the private sector where they would be directly impacted by the laws they helped to draft and pass. Our elected officials are there to represent the voters. When people stay in elected office for fifteen, twenty, twenty-five years or more, they become their own constituency, separate from other citizens. They become their own special interest group, lobbying us. We, of course, act as if we see them as a group we need to lobby rather than as our elected representatives. We have forgotten what Ross Perot often reminded us of—that our elected officials work for us.

Along with term limits, among the other election reform changes that ought to happen is one that most people, once they hear it explained, seem to be very enthusiastic about: compacting the votes on many offices and items into one voting day. For example, in New Jersey, there are separate voting days for the fire budget and the school budget. Wouldn't it make sense to hold these votes—and others, if possible—on the same day? And why not have voting days on weekends, when a greater number of people can get to the polls?

Election mechanics is an issue that also affects voters, and can provide protection from voter fraud. Voters should be asked to produce a voting card ID, as well as to sign in to match signatures. Currently, the New Jersey regulations say you may vote if you can present any one of the following: driver's license, student or job ID, military or other government ID, store membership, U.S. passport, bank statement, car registration, government check or document, sample ballot, utility bill, rent receipt, or an "other official document." This additional check would prevent double voting in more than one district (which does happen), and votes by people no longer on the voting lists. In addition, states ought to be more vigilant about keeping voting rolls up-to-date, promptly removing the names of people who have moved or died.

Another election issue UWSA members addressed in the mid-1990s was that of negative campaigning. Rather than highlighting a candidate's platform, campaign ads in recent decades focus more and more on attacking the opponent. This tactic doesn't educate voters about where candidates stand on the issues. Instead, the election focus becomes the personal background of candidates and making one's opponent look as bad as possible, while the candidates' qualifications and positions on issues become marginalized.

The Gallup Poll organization called the 2000 presidential election race between George W. Bush and Al Gore "one of the most negative presidential elections in recent history" (Negative Campaigning Disliked by Most Americans, July 17, 2000). And that contest pales in comparison with 2004 when President Bush and John Kerry spent a lot of political capital disparaging each other's military records. That this strategy is being used more often is surprising, since these attack ads are remembered by voters, the majority of whom are turned off by them. The above-referenced Gallup Poll found in 2000 that "three out of five Americans disagree with the idea that negative advertisements have a place in a campaign."

An additional element of election reform that has a major impact on the final election results is the role of the Electoral College. The creation of the Electoral College in 1787 has led to problems in some elections. For example, if you lose the popular vote in New York State by a margin of 49 percent to 51 percent, you get zero electoral votes, despite getting almost half of the popular vote. This has created the tendency for presidential nominees to focus their attention and visits on the states where they have the best chance to win all of the electoral votes, even if the popular election was close. This presidential election system actually allowed Al Gore to win the popular vote but lose the election to George W. Bush in 2000.

Members of UWSA continually discussed the Electoral College issue on line, in meetings, and in letters to the editor from 1993–95. Most members favored doing away with this mechanism because it appeared to be less democratic. Many members believed it was time to have a direct popular vote for president. The Electoral College, many believe, is an obsolete mechanism now that technology (provided it is not tampered with, of course) allows every vote to be counted quickly and accurately. Since 1944, polls have consistently shown by a heavy margin that the voters are in favor of the popular election of the president (*The Milford Massachusetts Daily News*. "Obsolete Electoral College." June 25, 2007). On the hopeful side, legislatures in New York, California, Massachusetts, and Maryland have voted to join an interstate compact to institute the direct popular election of the president, and many more states are expected to join them.

Another issue that I place into the election reform category is that of lobbying. If you think lobbying does not appear to play a role in elections, think again. For example, people who lobby our elected officials, and often actually write the legislation, spend millions of dollars helping candidates win elections. Additionally, union leaders and their members help get out the vote for candidates, as do members of large corporations who have a lot to gain from seeing the candidates they've lobbied or supported get elected.

Reform of the lobbying system is a complicated process that raises constitutional issues. But despite complexities—or perhaps because of them—the majority of UWSA members supported reform. Today, this issue still remains a concern, as lobbyists like Jack Abramoff are indicted for breaking laws and bribing elected officials, and some elected representatives (including Representative James Traficant (D-Ohio), Representative William Jefferson (D-Louisiana), Representative Tom DeLay (R-Texas), Representative Randy "Duke" Cunningham, (R-California)—need I go on?—are indicted or slink out of office under clouds of suspicion.

The final issue under the election reform umbrella is ballot access. Each state determines the requirements to be met by a candidate in order to appear on its ballot. Most require a certain number of signatures. Some states require paying fees from $2,000 to $7,500 in order to gain ballot access. Other states have low signature requirements, but control the election by directing where an alternative party candidate's name can physically appear on the ballot.

For example, in New Jersey, it only takes eight hundred signatures to get a candidate's name on the election ballot. However, each county in New Jersey (there are twenty-one counties) has the right to determine where to place the name of an alternative party's candidate. This means candidates cannot advertise statewide to let people know where on the ballot to find an independent or alternative party candidate's name when they go to vote. This boosts the cost of advertising, because separate ads must be produced for each county. In my experience, people at the voting booth become very confused when they try to find the name of the alternative party candidate, because placement varies from county to county and election to election.

I will come back to the ballot access issue in chapter 7.

Ross Perot's radio show

From April 1994 to June 1995, Ross Perot hosted a weekly radio show called *Listening to America* on which he addressed many of the previously discussed issues that had become the focus of UWSA members and citizens nationwide.

Each radio show opened with a dedication by Ross Perot. For example, on the March 12, 1995 program, Ross began, "Tonight's program is dedicated to the men and women who served our country in Somalia. As you know, our troops have just withdrawn from Somalia. Many Americans felt our troops should not have been there, but that's a completely separate issue from the fact that our troops carried out their orders and did a world class job under very difficult circumstances. Tonight, we welcome all of you home and we honor you for your service to our country."

After the dedication came the introduction of that night's political guest. These guests included many senators and congressional representatives. The following are among those who were guests on the show: Texas congressman Bill Archer, House Ways and Means Committee chairman; Georgia senator Sam Nunn, former Armed Services Committee chairman; New Mexico senator Pete Domenici, Senate Budget Committee chairman; Ohio congresswoman Marci Kaptur, strong anti-NAFTA member; Kansas senator Bob Dole, senate majority leader; Pennsylvania senator Arlen Spector; Texas senator Phil Gramm; Illinois senator Paul Simon, and many others.

The format of Perot's radio show included a short bio of the night's guest, followed by questions from the call-in audience. The topics raised by the listeners who called in included the Balanced Budget Amendment being discussed in Congress, tax reform, the idea of a flat tax, America's dependence on foreign oil, immigration and border security, education reform, the Oklahoma City bombing (many episodes addressed events that were happening at the time—1994 to 1995), health care reform, judicial reform, welfare reform, the trade deficit, and the national debt.

Once while I was listening to the program, one question and answer in particular caught my attention. A Florida University student addressed the question to Illinois senator Paul Simon.

CALLER:　　　　　　I have a comment and a question. The comment is actually a quote from "Atlantic Monthly." They stated that 65 representatives served four million Americans in the first Congress, a ratio of approximately 1 to 60,000. Today, with 435 representatives serving a population of more than 260 million, the ratio is approximately 1 to 600,000. Not related to my comment, my question is, Senator, what percentage of Senators and Representatives actually read the bills they sign?

SENATOR SIMON:　　Well, if you're talking about reading, and I'm not sure what that has to do with your first comment, in Illinois, for example, there are two senators and we represent about 12 million people. It varies a great deal in the Senate. But my staff goes over the bills and some of them I read personally. Some of them I take my staff's advice [people who are not elected by the voters] on. Some of them I rely on people in committees. That's why we have committees. Part of the answer to your question is we should be more careful and where it becomes a real problem, in particular, is when you get into conference between the House and the Senate. Then a bill comes from the conference committee and it is just not common at all that you have enough time to really study what you're voting on that comes from the conference committee.

I realized a lot about how our government works (or doesn't work!) from that exchange. And, I recalled De Clapsadle from Ohio telling us (UWSA members) that our elected representatives did not and could not read the more than one thousand pages of the NAFTA legislation! Don't you think this may explain why we're now having problems with industries and jobs leaving the United States in the steel industry, customer service, television and computer manufacturing, automobile manufacturing, production of apparel, and many other areas of the manufacturing sector?

Those who tuned in learned a tremendous amount about the actual inner workings (and shortcomings) of our government from Ross Perot's radio program.

The call-in questions and answers would go on for about an hour. Then Perot would close the show with a short story about an individual who was contributing to the lives of other Americans. The following is an example of one such tribute:

MR. PEROT: They met ten years ago at a Texas nursing home. Jim Newman, a retired engineer, who is now 86, had been coming there for two years to visit his wife who was in a coma. He spent nearly all day at her bedside. Before Mrs. Newman died, Jim got acquainted with a five-year-old boy named Michael Harris. He was mentally handicapped and had cerebral palsy. The two have been together nearly every day since. Says Mr. Newman "It means a lot to children to have someone to talk to them, even children that can't respond. They want attention and love. They really appreciate it."

In 1987, Michael, who is a ward of the state of Texas, was moved to a children's facility in northern Texas. Three days later, Mr. Newman packed his belongings and moved 320 miles to be near Michael. Mr. Newman said, "I just couldn't let him come up here by himself. Of course, my family thought I was crazy. I just closed my house and rented a room here."

Louise Marcum, administrator of this facility, said that she and her staff had been overwhelmed by Jim Newman's devotion to Michael. Fran Gratz, Michael's former teacher at Azle Jr. High School agrees. "There's a difference when Mr. Newman comes. Michael gets so excited and thrilled," she says. "He laughs and smiles and his eyes light up. There's just a different expression on his face."

Mr. Newman takes Michael for a ride in his wheelchair in the afternoons after classes. "I've gained as much out of it as he has," says Mr. Newman. "Anybody that looks after children gains from it." At the end of the day, Jim tucks Michael into bed. "I kiss him good night and tell him I'll be back tomorrow. I tell him I love him and that God loves him too."

Ross Perot concluded with, "Mr. Newman, you're a wonderful role model for us all. You live by the Golden Rule."

This radio program reflected the true spirit and patriotism of Ross Perot, as well as the mission and community of United We Stand America—the mission of political reform, and to establish a country run by its people to help its people.

The radio show also led to the next historic step in the ongoing communication between the people and their representatives—the August 1995 UWSA Conference, entitled "Preparing Our Country for the 21st Century."

Chapter 6

The UWSA Dallas Conference: Preparing Our Country for the 21st Century

Media reaction—David Broder

"On August 11–13, 1995, some of the country's greatest policy experts, legislators, and decision makers came together in Dallas, Texas, for an historic conference on the issues that confront Americans as we prepare for the future."

Most UWSA members and conference attendees agreed with David Broder's assessment, quoted above in the August 16, 1995 edition of the *Washington Post*. In his on-the-scene report, Broder stated, "[Conference attendees and those whom they represent] are the people who think our political system and parties have failed in their basic mission of channeling the people's commands to the organs of government. Millions of others who share that view have quit voting, have stopped following public affairs and have turned their backs on the responsibilities of citizenship.

"The Perot people share that disillusionment but instead of dropping out, they have stepped up their civic involvement. They have been moved to take action on their own to repair what they think is wrong.

"For that reason alone they deserve admiration.

"The attention that prominent Republicans and Democrats lavished on them last weekend was not misplaced. It was, if anything, a necessary plea from the political establishment to the people who may help save the system of self-government from the corrosive cynicism that is undermining it."

Diane McKelvey from Michigan was one of those people David Broder was talking about. She said, "I wonder how many people recognize the effort it took to get to this conference in Dallas. Mostly we are talking about middle-class working people and some students that had to take time off from work or school to attend."

Diane continued, "In my area we had a group of seven, and we had rented a large van from a major rental company. This would accommodate the people going and the luggage that they were bringing. We were planning to leave at 6 a.m. from my house and drive straight through to Dallas. Alec [Diane's husband] and I arrived at the rental office at about 6 p.m. the day before to pick up the van. Alas, this was not to be! I was informed that they didn't have a van and were very sorry. However, they offered to give us two cars at the same price. This was not workable since we only had three drivers and one couldn't drive at night. We checked with all of the other rental agencies and there was just no van available. Then panic set in!"

Alec came to the rescue, as Diane explained, "Alec recalled that his daughter had a van—a mini van. An OLD mini van. Desperation prompted a phone call to her to see if she could do without the van for several days. She gladly let us use it."

She went on, "The rest of the story is worthy of the keystone cops. We stacked seven people and all of the luggage into that mini van and drove the 23 hours to Dallas! Was it worth it? You bet!"

Diane expressed the sentiments of many who attended. She said, "The conference was amazing with the powerhouse speakers. I can't recall the number of times the audience members were brought to their feet cheering and clapping for the issues that were at the forefront of our philosophy. I need to mention that the audience was also gracious to those we did not agree with. I don't recall a 'boo' at any time."

She stated, "It was here that an important piece of my political education took place. I was in awe of the 'important' people I met and spoke with. I was interviewed by several well-known newscasters and had several conversations with Jesse Jackson, Pat Buchanan, Linda Smith (who was terrific), and even Al Franken! It was here that it finally dawned on me that these were only people. People like myself, but in positions of influence. I realized that they were interested in me. Not because I was individually important, but because I was part of a group that was greatly influencing that political scene."

Diane and the other UWSA attendees, the speakers, the workshop participants, and all the people who helped to organize and run this conference were part of a political phenomenon the likes of which to this point had never occurred in the twentieth century.

As Ross Perot stated in the Vol. 3, No. 7, (September 1995) issue of the United We Stand America national newsletter, "The thousands of United We Stand America members who were able to attend the National Conference gave a clear and unmistakable message to the leaders of both political parties and the [1996] Presidential candidates—We are the owners of this country. We want to be informed on the issues that face this great nation. We will work tirelessly to find sensible solutions to our country's problems."

Appearing in this same newsletter was an article by UWSA member David C. Trussell in which he summed up the feelings of many attendees. Mr. Trussell stated, "'Unprecedented' was the word used by many members of the media in describing the UWSA National Conference. The thousands of people sitting in the arena of the Dallas Convention Center knew they were taking part in history.

"Critics called the conference a 'panderama' for GOP presidential hopefuls, but they conveniently ignored the long list of speakers who were not looking for votes. These speakers brought a diverse array of political views."

The speakers and their topics

Speakers addressing the issue of government reform included former senator David Boren from Oklahoma. Additionally, Congresswoman Linda Smith from the state of Washington and Congressman Sam Brownback [now Senator] from Kansas spoke about campaign finance reform and lobbying reform.

Senator Pete Domenici from New Mexico, Congressman John Kasich from Ohio, and Senator Paul Simon from Illinois spoke about government spending and taxes. Meredith Bagby, a recent Harvard graduate, presented *The First Annual Report of The United States of America*.

The Reverend Jesse Jackson spoke about jobs and "The Ladder of Opportunity." Congresswoman Marcy Kaptur from Ohio, who voted against the North American Free Trade Agreement, discussed the critical importance of keeping manufacturing jobs in the United States.

One of the most enthusiastic audience responses was reserved for Congresswoman Kaptur, recalled Donna Donovan, who came from Connecticut for the conference. Donna pointed out one particular paragraph from Kaptur's speech in the transcript of the conference, in which she talked about the impact of NAFTA. It reads:

> What happened to Linda LaChance of Biddeford, Maine, describes part of our current quandary. In 1979, Linda earned $10 an hour making shoes in Nike's last shoe plant in America. In 1985, six years later, Nike moved her job and thousands of others overseas. Since then, Linda has been unemployed three times. Today, she's making $5.50 an hour. As Linda says, "Nike's motto is 'Just Do It.' Well, they did it to me." Nike now manufactures 100% of its shoes overseas, using 30,000 contract laborers in China and Asia, paying them 30 cents an hour. It costs Nike $8 to make a pair of shoes, which they then ship back to us and charge us $69.99 to $150 a pair. Then, Nike paid Michael Jordan $20 million for advertising campaigns to

make us feel good about Nike, while Nike pocketed $3.8 billion in revenues in 1994, and Phil Knight, its Chief Executive Officer, smiled all the way to the bank with his $3/4 million salary, plus $718,000 in bonus and stock options. Is this what we want for America?

During the next break in the conference presentations, Donna recalled, "I went outside for some fresh air. Right outside the door, someone had left their Nike sneakers with a note tucked in front of them that said the owner didn't want them any more, and wouldn't buy Nike until the company started making their products in the United States again. By the end of the break, there was a pretty good pile of discarded sneakers there, as others from the audience joined the Perot/Kaptur chorus!"

Pete Peterson made another well-received address. He is the founding president of the Concord Coalition, a nonprofit organization focused on economic problems in America such as the budget deficit and the growing cost of entitlements. His topic was "The Silent Crisis in Social Security."

Three conference speakers, including Governor Tommy Thompson of Wisconsin, who later would serve under President George W. Bush as secretary of health and human services from 2001 to 2005, discussed health care.

Congresswoman Barbara Jordan of Texas, now deceased, gave a moving presentation on immigration reform. Her message carries even more urgency today.

Senator Sam Nunn from Georgia addressed the "Responsibilities of the World's Last Superpower."

Political party leaders representing the Democrats at the conference included the counselor to President Bill Clinton, Mack McLarty; Connecticut senator Chris Dodd; House Democratic Leader Dick Gephardt; and Senate Minority Leader Tom Daschle. Republican political leaders present included Chairman of the Republican National Committee Haley Barbour (who is now governor of Mississippi), Speaker of the House Newt Gingrich, and Senate Majority Whip Trent Lott. Also, nine 1996 presidential candidates spoke, including Senator Bob Dole, Senator Arlen Specter, Senator Phil Gramm, Pat Buchanan, and Alan Keyes.

The official transcript of the United We Stand America conference was published in paperback in 1995 under the title *Preparing Our Country for the 21st Century* by the Harper Collins division HarperPerennial. The book includes all of the speeches given at the conference, any of which could be given today with as much, if not more, critical relevance.

In his UWSA newsletter review of the conference, David Trussell pointed out that "The slate of speakers provided clear evidence that leadership ability is not determined by race, gender, or age, and that, as Ross Perot has often said, America's diversity is one of its greatest strengths" (*United We Stand America—The National Newsletter.* Vol. 3, No. 7. September 1995).

Workshops and issue booths

The conference also featured issue booths where people could get information and sign petitions to support the legislation they favored. I spent time working at the campaign finance reform (CFR) booth where people could find out about a bill (HR 2072) sponsored by Washington Congresswoman Linda Smith. This bill requires candidates to raise their contributions only from within the state they wished to represent, limited political campaigning to no more than three months before an election, and established Saturday and Sunday for election voting. Other items addressed lobbying reform and term limits (*United We Stand America Newsletter*. Vol. 3, No. 7. September 1995). After Representative Smith's presentation on campaign finance reform, a line of about one hundred people formed at our booth to sign a petition in support of her CFR bill.

In addition, workshops on various issues were open to the conference attendees. Social Security, health care, balancing the federal budget, term limits, trade, creating jobs in the United States, and campaign finance reform were some of the issues addressed in these meetings.

I participated in the CFR workshop along with Representative Smith. The workshop panelists presented different points of view on how to reduce the money thrown at political campaigns. Their solutions ranged from public financing to individual contributions only from the people who were eligible to vote for each individual candidate.

California UWSA member Judy Duffy's comments summed up most members' views on the workshops when she said, "I thought the outline and the speakers were very good. It was so clear which [speakers] were just giving us the same ol' line and [which] ones [came] with a real message or at least felt strongly about where they stood [on the issues].

"The workshops and breakouts were very impressive as we finally saw some real great ideas and consensus on many of the issues with people that were well spoken and had thoughtful ideas."

Impact of the conference

The conference was also viewed by millions of people at home watching CNN and C-SPAN, and it was reported on by all of the major networks. Larry King and other television news and talk show hosts broadcast live from the conference hall.

The vast majority of responses I received from viewers were positive. These people, like most attendees, expressed the hope that our elected representatives would finally listen to the people who elected them. After all, they said, the politicians work for us.

This conference proved that *issue forums work*. However, we also learned it takes time and money to produce issue forums, including teams of volunteers who are committed to an educated electorate and a truly working democracy.

In addition, something else happened at this conference that led to a new groundswell of supporters. UWSA members from fourteen states had gotten together and decided they wanted to use another tool to "restore integrity to our political system"(*United We Stand America Newsletter*. Vol. 3, No. 7. September 1995). These states' attendees wanted to create a political party alternative to the Democrats and Republicans.

From August 1995 through the November 1996 election, UWSA and a third party that was to become the Reform Party coexisted. Many people participated in both entities.

Media coverage increased dramatically

Interestingly, UWSA now received more media coverage than it had in the past. For example, on August 28, 1995, the *Wall Street Journal* ran a front-page article by John Harwood. Mr. Harwood addressed the growing "widespread distrust" and disillusionment spreading across America. He said, "What is striking about the discontent among U.S. voters now is how widely it is shared: roughly six in ten Democrats say the country is headed in the wrong direction; six in ten Republicans and Independents say the same thing, according to a recent survey by Democratic pollster Stan Greenberg and Republican counterpart Fred Steeper."

John Harwood pointed out, "Some frustrated voters are moving to take the issue into their own hands.... Ms. Benjamin wants to empower fellow New Jerseyians with information. So with the help of her computer-savvy husband and a small committee of United We Stand volunteers, she [plus 40 additional UWSA volunteers] has painstakingly entered into her own [UWSA's] database some 18,000 pages of campaign finance reports [from 1993] of state legislators. The data will help voters track debates in Trenton, she says because 'the people who give them the money are going to determine which budget goes through.' ... Republican [and Democratic] luminaries joined the Benjamins and other Perotistas [at the UWSA national conference] in Dallas and maintained that they are interested in political reform, too. Ms. Benjamin's attitude is simple: 'Show me.' ... She says of politicians: 'We don't trust them. There's a disconnect between what the public thinks change is, and what the people in office think. I know it hasn't happened yet.'"

The UWSA New Jersey campaign finance reform project discussed in John Harwood's *Wall Street Journal* article was presented to the New Jersey media at a press conference on September 13, 1995. The 1993 New Jersey State Legislature campaign contributions were broken down by percentage and contributing entities, with the realtors leading the nonpolitical PAC contributions. Also included was a separate study of one town, Gloucester Township in Camden County, New Jersey. This report, presented in the previous chapter, clearly demonstrated a direct relationship between awarded contracts and 1994 local campaign contributions.

The media coverage in New Jersey generated by the Dallas conference continued through the September 1995 Campaign Finance presentation all the way until the UWSA New Jersey Annual State Conference which took place on October 28, 1995 at the Hyatt Regency in New Brunswick, New Jersey. The agenda for this meeting, which indicates all of the issues important to the people of New Jersey, can be found in figure 6.1.

UNITED WE STAND AMERICA
New Jersey Annual State Conference

PROGRAM

9:00 a.m.	**Conference Opening Remarks** Norris Clark UWSA-NJ Executive Director	**11:45 a.m.**	**Lunch**
9:15 a.m.	**Education Reform** Mayor Bret Schundler Duane Warehime UWSA-NJ Education Team Leader Question and Answer	**12:45 p.m.** **1:00 p.m.**	**Afternoon Introduction** Norris Clark **Republican Agenda for NJ Assembly Races** Steve Corodemus Republican Majority Whip Question and Answer
10:10 a.m.	**Trade and Jobs** Rick Engler NJ Industrial Union Council, AFL-CIO Pete Robison UWSA-NJ Trade Team Leader Question and Answer		**Democratic Agenda for NJ Assembly Races** B. Thomas Byrne, Jr. NJ Democratic Party Chair Question and Answer
11:00 a.m.	**Campaign Finance Reform** Congresswoman Linda Smith Pat Benjamin UWSA-NJ Campaign Finance Reform Team Leader Question and Answer		**NJ Conservative Party Agenda for NJ Assembly Races** Tom Blomquist NJ Conservative Party Founder Question and Answer
		3:00 p.m.	**Ross Perot**

October 28, 1995 • Hyatt Regency • New Brunswick, NJ

Page 1 New Jersey Reform Party Annual State conference

The UWSA-NJ executive director, Norris Clark, opened the New Jersey conference. He was followed by many speakers, including Jersey City mayor Bret Schundler, on education reform; Rick Engler, AFL-CIO representative, on trade and jobs; Congresswoman Linda Smith, on campaign finance reform; and the three UWSA team leaders—Duane Warehime, leader of the UWSA education team; Pete Robison, UWSA-NJ trade team leader; and myself, UWSA-NJ campaign finance reform team leader. Also speaking were the Democrat, Republican, and New Jersey Conservative Party leaders on the upcoming New Jersey Assembly races. The conference closed with a presentation by Ross Perot.

The Dallas conference had also given UWSA members from across the country the chance to meet with our elected Washington representatives, and led to meetings in Washington and input into reform legislation sponsored by these Dallas conference speakers.

After the Dallas conference, I was appointed campaign finance reform national team leader. With Russell Verney, UWSA national chairman, I met with John McCain's team to discuss this issue. In addition, I worked with Bob Franks, New Jersey congressman and Linda Smith, Washington congresswoman to support the Bipartisan Clean Congress Act. Sadly, this bill was never allowed to face a vote on the floor of Congress because it threatened the campaign system that helped incumbents—who are the same people who would vote on this bill! Talk about the fox guarding the hen house!

Even so, the August 1995 UWSA national conference in Dallas had increased the visibility of the issues UWSA members supported, as well as the role of United We Stand America in raising public awareness of these issues.

However, as I alluded to earlier, many UWSA members felt that the UWSA issues organization was being impeded by not creating a mechanism to help reformers get elected to local office or sit in state legislatures and in Congress. They believed we were still too dependent on the Republicans and Democrats and needed our own elected representatives to get bills passed into law.

In 1995 and 1996, UWSA members continued to visit Congress, state legislatures, local officials, and to reach out to citizen voters. Our activity increased, and so did the press coverage.

At the same time that UWSA was having a major impact on the government, those who supported the development of a new political party created the Committee to Establish the Reform Party (CERP). They began the long, tedious, and expensive process of placing a presidential candidate's name on the ballot in all fifty states.

Chapter 7

The Birth of the Reform Party

United We Stand America continued full steam through November 1996. However, at the same time, the Committee to Establish the Reform Party (CERP) had been organized, and voter signatures were being collected in states across the country to place our presidential nominee on each state ballot.

In addition, new people who had not participated in UWSA were joining the Reform Party. Many of these people had supported Perot for president in 1992 and had then chosen not to join UWSA. They believed in the need to form alternative political parties, such as the Patriot Party, the New Alliance Party, the Independence Party, a Connecticut organization known as A Connecticut Party, and others. Once the decision was made to create the Reform Party, many of the members of other alternative parties left to join the Perot-inspired Reform Party.

Jim Mangia was one of those people. Looking back at 1996, he recalls, "I was the California Chairperson of the Patriot Party and the Executive Committee voted to become part of the Reform Party the day after Ross Perot made his announcement on Larry King Live. I met with Russ Verney [chairman of CERP] and we did a joint press conference announcing that the Patriot Party would contact its 10,000 registrants [in California] and urge them to re-register into the Reform Party and that our party activists around the state would participate in the Reform Party drive. This received major coverage in the Los Angeles Times. We registered several thousand more in those eighteen days [that we had to qualify for the California 1996 presidential election ballot.] Once we succeeded we had a meeting ... in West Los Angeles and developed an interim

Board of Directors of the key activists who had led the drive. I was elected Secretary of the California Reform Party."

Meanwhile, new party participants were beginning to unravel the incredibly complex snarl of ballot access rules and regulations (for what were termed "minor party candidates") put in place by state legislators.

Ballot access

Each state controls the candidate's ability to get his or her name on the ballot for any elected office, and each state has its own rules and regulations. This makes it very difficult and expensive for independent candidates or candidates nominated by an alternative (neither Democrat nor Republican) political party to gain ballot access.

State requirements—expensive and confusing

Examples of how difficult it is to get an independent or alternative party candidate on the ballot are many, and very little has changed in the past decade to make the process easier. In California, for a 2004 statewide office, 1 percent or 153,805 signatures were required on a petition to put a non-major-party candidate on the election ballot. According to the requirements, circulation of signature petitions must take place between 193 and 88 days before the election. A second alternative was to get more than 100,000 voters to change their registration to the alternative party. The Reform Party used the second option because the members were told by the California secretary of state that it was too late to use the first option. This means that a large candidate organization was (and still is) required throughout the state, which again means the need for plenty of money to cover the cost of signature collectors.

In the 1990s in Pennsylvania, 2,000 signatures were required to place any candidate on the election ballot. In 2006, approximately 67,000 signatures were needed for an independent or alternative party candidate—thirty-three times more than for a Democrat or Republican.

In Ohio in 1996, a problem arose during the petitioning to put Ross Perot's name on the presidential ballot. Mike Hicks, initially a volunteer who was then hired by the Perot team because of his computer expertise, was sent to address the Ohio problem. According to Hicks, "Despite an overwhelming number of petitions, the Ohio Secretary of State Bob Taft [who went on to become Ohio's governor in 1999 and who was convicted of criminal charges in 2006 for accepting gifts and related ethics violations] denied the validity of the petition signatures and rejected the ballot access for Ross Perot and the Reform Party. So, I [Mike] went to Ohio the following week to prove we had enough signatures. [Ohio ballot] access required 45,000 and the state claimed we had less than 40,000.

"I arrived in Columbus, rented computers, set up a network, installed a database package, and began purchasing voter registration files. I hired temporary workers who checked every petition page, identifying which signatures were good. We began finding valid signatures that had been disqualified by the county employees who checked the petitions for the counties.

"Some counties were cooperative, none were supportive, and some were clearly opposed to seeing [the Reform Party] succeed. I remember sitting in the office of the election officer in Montgomery county, Ohio, and being told 'Mike, I don't appreciate your coming in here and questioning the work of my team. I think it best that you just get the hell out of Montgomery County.'

"Needless to say, I personally checked every signature from Montgomery County, guessing based on his remarks and attitude that I would find a larger percentage of falsely denied signatures from Montgomery County. This proved true. There were many obviously valid petition signatures that were marked as invalid in that county.

"Bob Taft's lack of support was not surprising, but was noticed. He could have easily provided me with the voter registration records for the entire state of Ohio, but refused to assist. I had to purchase the records in different formats, on different media types from each county, often with unexplained two- and three-week delays. It was suggested several times to me by workers in the counties that the 'off the record' directive from both political parties was to slow the Perot effort as much as possible.

"We began a weekly process of sitting with Taft's staff and challenging signatures.... Delays were the order of the day. Once it became clear that we were going to prove we had the required number of signatures, they quietly granted us ballot access."

In Maine, signatures were turned in on December 14, 1995, to Maine secretary of state Bill Diamond (now a state senator) for Reform Party ballot access in 1996. On January 4, 1996, Secretary Diamond rejected the Reform Party petition claiming the number of signatures certified at that time was short 515 valid signatures from the 25,565 signatures required by law. Since the Maine Reform Party signature collectors had kept copies of the material, they went to court to overturn the secretary of state's decision. They named Secretary Diamond and selected municipal registrars as defendants. "On March 21, 1996, the municipal registrars acknowledged that at least 520 signatures were incorrectly rejected. Following this agreement, Secretary Diamond said a change in the law would be necessary to officially recognize the Reform Party in Maine.... The Maine State Legislature voted overwhelmingly to acknowledge that the Reform Party [had] qualified for the state's 1996 ballot. Maine Governor Angus King (an Independent) signed the bill into law on April 5, 1996. The bill, introduced by State Minority Leader Mark Lawrence (Democrat) at the request of Secretary of State Bill Diamond, followed and agreement between Reform Party organizers and seven municipal voter registrars that the petition filed on December 14, 1995 did, in fact, have sufficient signatures to meet state requirements" (*United We Stand America Newsletter*. Vol. 4, No. 3. April 1996).

In 2007, eleven years later, many state ballot access requirements continue to make it difficult for independent candidates and alternative party candidates to run for office throughout the United States.

As the ballot access specialist Richard Winger pointed out in his August 1, 2006 issue of *Ballot Access News*, "New Mexico is the only state that requires one petition to qualify the party, and then *separate* petitions for each nominee. New Mexico has required 'double petitioning' since 1979, and no one has ever sued to overturn it."

Mr. Winger also points out, "New Hampshire is the only New England state that has not had any qualified third parties during the past ten years."

Debra Schneider of New Jersey, who prepared the following chart of the fifty state petition signature and/or filing fee requirements, noted the difficulty of understanding each state's constantly changing ballot access laws. The data for the following chart came from the Reform Institute Web site, located at www.reforminstitute.org.

Petition Signature Requirements	Petition Signature Requirements	Filing Fee Requirements	Filing Fee Requirements	Filing Fee Requirements
State (Major, Minor, Established, Recognized)	Independent or New Party	Democrats	Republican	Independent

This chart is an abbreviated overview to show how the requirements vary from state to state. Even the definitions of candidates other than Democrats and Republican vary widely. Also, not every state has a primary election. If it does, Third Party candidates may be excluded from the primary process and have to meet a different set of state requirements to get on the general election ballot.

This information was extracted from The Reform Institute. For more information, or information specific to your state, go to www.reforminstiture.org

In Pennsylvania, the rules for Independents require them to obtain signatures from registered voters equal to 2% of the highest vote getter in the last statewide election. In 2004, the highest vote getter was state Treasurer Bob Casey, Jr. who got over 3.3 million votes. So, 67,070 signatures needed in order to get on the November 7 ballot. Pennsylvania has a Ballot Access Coalition who is trying to address this issue through the Voters' Choice Act. To download the Voters' Choice Act and its accompanying white paper, go to: www.PABallotAccess.org

First Page of State Ballot Access Charts

State	Petition Signature Requirements (Major, Minor, Established, Recognized)	Petition Signature Requirements Independent or New Party	Filing Fee Requirements Democrats	Filing Fee Requirements Republican	Filing Fee Requirements Independent
AL	500 signatures total or 50 signatures from each congressional district	5,000	$2,000	$5,000	$0
AK	After the national convention the party's nat'l committee notifies the Secy of State of its candidates	1 % of all votes cast in the previous presidential election for minor party candidates. No procedure to get on ballot other than forming a minor party			$0
AZ	File a nomination paper with the Secy of State	File a nomination paper with the Secy of State. Petition 3% of voters statewide	$1,000	$0	$0
AR	**Democrat:** 3% of votes in previous presidential primary or 1,000 per congressional district, whichever is less. **Republican:** none	3% of voters in previous presidential primary or 1,000 per congressional district, whichever is less.	$0	$0	$0
CA	Secy of State selects party candidates. If not selected:Democratic: 1% of registered voters or 500 in ea of the 53 congressional districts whichever is fewer. **All other parties:** 1 % of registered voters statewide	To qualify, a group of 55 presidential electors who pledge their votes to the nominee. Petition, 1 %of registered voters statewide	$2,500	$10,000	$0
CO	Must qualify for federal presidential primary matching payment. 5,000 signatures OR filing fee (Minor candidates have different qualifiers)	File a statement of intent with Secy of State. 5,000 **signatures OR filing fee**	$500	$500	$500
CT (I)	Secy of State selects candidates. If not selected: 1% of registered party voters. Minor party: received 1 % of votes cast for president in the previous election	1 % of turnout at last presidential election or 7,500 signatures whichever is less	$0	$0	$0

Second Page of State Ballot Access Charts

State	Petition Signature Requirements (Major, Minor, Established, Recognized) Independent	Petition Signature Requirements Independent or New Party	Filing Fee Requirements Democrats	Filing Fee Requirements Republican	Filing Fee Requirements Independent
DE	**Qualify** for Presidential Party Matching funds, or 500 signatures, file with Secy of State. Minor party nomination results submitted to State Election Comm.	Sworn Declaration. 1 % of total number of registered voters from previous year			$0
FL	Affiliated with a national party holding a national convention. 1 %of the registered electors of the state.	1% of registered electors in the state	$0	$0	$0
GA	**Major:** party submits a list of candidates to appear on the primary ballot to Secy of State. **Minor:** 1 % of total votes from precious presidential election	File notice of candidacy, petition 1 % total votes from previous **presidential** election			$0
HI	One tenth of registered voters	1 % of votes cast in previous presidential election	$1,500	$0	$0
ID	Secy of State selects candidates. If not selected: 1 % of registered party voters. Minor party: State party chairman submits candidate names to the Secy of State	New Party; 2% of the vote. Independent: 1 % pf votes in previous presidential election	$0	$0	$0
IL	3,000-5,000 signatures	1 % of voters or 25,000 signatures	$0	$0	$0
IN	4,500 signatures including 500 from each congressional district	2% of votes cast in the most recent election for Secy of State (2)	$0	$0	$0
IA	Received at least 2% of the vote for governor or president in the last general election	**Minor & Independent: 1,500 signatures in not less than 10 counties**	$0	$0	$0
KS	2% of the last vote for Secy of State OR received at least 5 % of the vote in the last gubernatorial election for parties that nominate by primaries rather than convention	5,000 signatures	$0	$0	$0

Third Page of State Ballot Access Charts

State	Petition Signature Requirements (Major, Minor, Established, Recognized)	Petition Signature Requirements Independent or New Party	Filing Fee Requirements Democrats	Filing Fee Requirements Republican	Filing Fee Requirements Independent
KY	5,000 signatures of registered voters of the same political party	5,000 signatures of registered voters statewide	$1,000	$1,000	$500
LA	1,000 signatures	5,000 signatures with 500 from each congressional district	$0	$5,000	$500
ME	2,000-3,000 signatures OR filing fee	4,000-6,000 signatures	$2,500	$2,500	$0
MD	(Secy of State selects) 400 signatures from ea of the 8 congressional districts	New Party: 10,000 signatures Independent: 1 % of registered voters	$0	$0	$0
MA	(Secy of State selects) 2,500 signatures statewide	10,000 signatures	$0	$0	$0
MI	(Secy of state OR state party chair submits names) 1/2 of 1 % of total votes cast in the state in the last presidential election not to exceed 1,000 times the number of congressional districts in the state	1 % of votes cast for all candidates for governor in the last election including 100 signatures from at least half of the congressional districts	$0	$0	$0
MN	5% of the total number of individuals who voted in the preceding state general election. **Minor:** received at least 1 % of the votes in each county	1 % of the total number of voters in the preceding general election OR 2,000 signatures whichever is less	$0	$0	$0
MS	(Secy of State selects) 500 signatures statewide or 100 from each congressional district	1,000 signatures	$0	$0	$0
Mo	Polled 2% in the two consecutive preceding general elections	New Party: 10,000 signatures (3) Independent: 10,000 signatures	$1,000	$1,000	$0

Fourth Page of State Ballot Access Charts

State	Petition Signature Requirements (Major, Minor, Established, Recognized)	Petition Signature Requirements Independent or New Party	Filing Fee Requirements Democrats	Filing Fee Requirements Republican	Filing Fee Requirements Independent
MT	Eligible for Matching Funds, file declaration of candidacy with the Secy of State, OR 500 signatures.	Non-recognized: req the primary election and signed by voters = to 5% or more of the total votes cast for the successful candidate for governor at the last general election OR 5,000 electors whichever is less which must include the voters in more than 1/3 of the legislative districts = to 5% or more of the total votes cast for the successful candidate for governor at the last general election OR 150 electors in those districts, whichever is less.			$0
NE	(Secy of State selects) 100 signatures of registered party voters in ea of the 3 districts	New Party & Independent: 2,500 signatures	$0	$0	$0
NV	Have 10% of the total number of registered voters in the state OR petition 10% of the total number of votes cast at the last preceding general election for the offices of Rep in Congress. Recognized Minor party qualifications: 1 % of the total number of votes cast at the last preceding general election for the office of Rep of Congress	1 % of votes cast in the previous election for US Rep	$0	$0	$250
NH	$1,000 OR 10 signatures from ea of the 21 counties	3,000 signatures, (1,500 from each of the two congressional districts)	$1,000	$1,000	$250
NJ	1,000 signatures	800 signatures	$0	$0	$0
NM	(Secy of State) 2% of the total number of votes for president cast in ea congressional district in the last presidential election	3% of statewide votes from the previous presidential election	$0	$0	$0

Fifth Page of State Ballot Access Charts

State	Petition Signature Requirements (Major, Minor, Established, Recognized)	Petition Signature Requirements Independent or New Party	Filing Fee Requirements Democrats	Filing Fee Requirements Republican	Filing Fee Requirements Independent
NY	5,000 signatures, Minor: 15,000 signatures	15,000 signatures, at least 100 must come from each of the 16 congressional districts	$0	$0	$0
NC	Received 10% of state votes cast in previous presidential election, or 2% of votes cast in most recent gubernatorial election	2% of registered voters statewide	$0	$0	$0
ND	Established: had printed on the ballot the last presidential election the names of presidential electors or a candidate for governor AND those candidates received at least 5% of the total vote cast for those offices	Third party: 7,000 signatures; Independent: 4,000 signatures	$0	$0	$0
OH	Major: candidate for governor or nominees For presidential electors at the most recent regular state election received at least 20% of the votes cast for that office. Intermediate or Minor: May submit names for president, VP and 20 presidential electors to the Secy of State	5,000 signatures	$0	$0	$0
OK	5% of the votes in the last gubernatorial election or received 10% of the votes cast in any general election	3% of the votes cast in the previous presidential election. Unrecognized parties must notify the Secy of State before circulating petitions (not required for independents)	$0	$0	$0
OR	(Secy of state selects) 1,000 signatures from each of the 5 congressional districts including signatures from the voters in 5% of the precincts in at least 1/4 of the counties in the district. Minor: 1.5 % of the total votes cast for governor	1 % of all votes cast in the previous presidential election (and prior approval from the Secy of State)	$0	$0	$0

Sixth Page of State Ballot Access Charts

State	Petition Signature Requirements (Major, Minor, Established, Recognized)	Petition Signature Requirements Independent or New Party	Filing Fee Requirements Democrats	Filing Fee Requirements Republican	Filing Fee Requirements Independent
PA	Only Democrats and Republicans can run in the primary. 2,000 signatures (100 from each of the 10 counties). Minor parties: Has less than 15% of registered voters statewide but had a candidate on previous ballot who polled more than 2% of the votes	Minor & Independent: 2% of the votes of the highest vote-getter in the previous election	$200	$200	$200
RI	5% of the entire vote cast for presidential or governor	1,000 signatures	$0	$0	$0
SC	Certified: 10,000 signatures Republicans: file a request with the state chair to appear on ballot Democrats: petition of candidacy to state party	10,000 signatures	$2,500	$10,000	$0
SD	2.5 % of votes cast for governor in the last general election	1 % of the total votes for governor in the previous election	$0	$0	$0
TN	Only Republican & Democrats recognized parties	New party: 2.5% of all votes cast in the previous gubernatorial election Independents: Secure 1 to 11 candidates for run as electors and ea elector circulates own petition for 25 signatures OR a master petition is circulated for all electors- 275 signatures	$0	$0	$0
TX	State chair of ea party certifies the name of ea presidential candidate to secy of State. Democrats: 5,000 signatures Republicans: 300 voters from the 15 congressional districts	1 % of votes cast in previous presidential election	$2,500	$4,000	$0
UT	2,000 signatures	1,000 signatures	$0	$2,500	$0

Seventh Page of State Ballot Access Charts

State	Petition Signature Requirements (Major, Minor, Established, Recognized)	Petition Signature Requirements Independent or New Party	Filing Fee Requirements Democrats	Filing Fee Requirements Republican	Filing Fee Requirements Independent
VT	Recd 5% of the votes for a statewide party candidate - $2,000 fee - if cannot pay, can file an affidavit and all but the $300 can be waived by Secy of State. 1,000 signatures	1,000 signatures	$2,000	$2,000	$0
VA	10,000 signatures of qualified voters who attest they intend to participate in the same primary as candidate, including 400 from ea of the 11 districts (but 700 from ea district is recommended)	10,000 signatures of qualified voters with 400 from ea district (it is recommended that 15,000 - 20,000 signatures be obtained with at least 700 from ea district			
WA	(Secy of state selects) 1,000 signatures	200 voters	$0	$0	$0
WV	1% of annual salary or 4 signatures for every dollar of filing fee if unable to pay	2% of total votes cast preceding presidential election for that party's candidate	1 % annual sal	1 % annual sal	1 % annual sal
WI	Pres Selection Comm selects major party candidates. 1,000 signatures from ea of the 8 districts but not more than 1,500	between 2,000 and 4,000 signatures	$0	$0	$0
WY	Petition with Secy of State or received 2% of the votes in the last gubernatorial Secy of State or US House of Rep election	2 % of the votes cast for US Rep in the last general election.	$0	$0	$0

(1) For purpose of the presidential primary only party means political party with the largest or second largest enrollment in the state

(2) In 2002 this was 30,716 signatures and only one candidate succeeded in getting on the ballot, Pat Buchanan of the Reform Party

(3) If after the first election the party wins more than 2% of the vote it becomes an established party. If does not poll over 2%, established status is lost.

Eighth Page of State Ballot Access Charts

Americans must continue to fight for equitable and understandable ballot access requirements in every state. By making access to the election ballot easier and less expensive for independent candidates, newly formed or alternative political parties, and non-major-party candidates, we will increase candidate choices and increase participation by the American public. It is patently obvious by now that this is not what entrenched political parties want. But the American people are entitled to nothing less.

Signature collection—the process and methods

In most states, collection of voter signatures is required in order to gain ballot access and to qualify a candidate's name for inclusion on an election ballot.

As mentioned earlier, state officials make the decision on how many signatures are required for Democrats, Republicans, independents, and alternative political parties.

Working to satisfy ballot access and signature requirements for independent or so-called "minor or unrecognized party" candidates requires an extensive, well-financed organization. These requirements, of course, limit the candidate choices for American voters. However, in the case of the newly formed Reform Party in 1995–96, Ross Perot provided capital to fund the signature collection process.

Different methods were used throughout the country to obtain voter signatures, and many volunteer teams got creative with their techniques. For example, in Connecticut, volunteers stood outside of stores and in other public places with a row of signature forms on clipboards placed on ironing boards with signs like "Let's iron out our country's problems." Donna Donovan said, "The boards were easy to transport, put the petitions at eye level, and attracted the attention and curiosity of the people going by."

In Arkansas, members independently arrived at the same idea of using an ironing board. According to Tom O'Brien, a field coordinator, "I worked in parts of Arkansas to get the party on the ballot in December 1995. In the cold of winter, I stood outside chicken-plucking factories with ironing boards trying to gather signatures. It was incredible to me to be standing at the gates of these factories every morning as the shift workers filtered in. These hardworking people would first laugh at us for having ironing boards standing out in the parking lot at 6:00 a.m., which would make them curious enough to ask what we were doing. When telling them we were going to get a new political party on the ballot so that they would have a chance at another candidate for president, nothing else seemed to matter. They would sign, wish us luck and tell their friends to do the same."

In Alaska, because of the cold weather, supporters could only collect signatures in places where the business owners allowed them indoors.

Most state Reform Party supporters found themselves collecting signatures in front of supermarkets and retail stores. Some malls allowed them in, while others forced them into parking lots or out of the entire mall area. Location depended on the laws and often the whim of the state, the business owners, and political election officials.

In Michigan, Diane McKelvey continued her political education, saying about the 1996 petition drive, "When I started out carrying petitions for the Reform Party, I thought it would be a walk in the park. Well it wasn't as easy as it was in 1992. I was not prepared for the partisan reaction. Some people were downright rude and would almost physically push me away. Others had many questions that they asked before they would sign. Some would sign immediately when they found out Perot was involved."

A number of Reform Party volunteer supporters and signature collectors were also Perot employees. They and other volunteers traveled from state to state helping to get the signatures required for qualification on each state's presidential election ballot.

In some states, such as Connecticut, all of the signatures were collected by state volunteers. In many states, money was needed to hire temporary workers as signature collectors in order to meet the tight state ballot access deadlines.

In order to keep track of each state's ballot access and signature requirements, Mike Morris, operations manager for the Committee to Establish the Reform Party, became project coordinator. He set up a nationwide chart to track the progress and follow the timeline so that all state deadlines were successfully met. This might mean sending additional people into states that were short-staffed, hiring additional temporary workers when and where needed, and sending people to address problems like those that occurred in Ohio and Maine, as detailed above.

Deadlines were met and the problems were addressed and solved. But, it took a strong commitment to the process, and an enormous investment of people, money, and time.

After her experiences in the petition drive, Diane McKelvey made the following observations: "1) Democrats were more willing to sign because they believed the Reform Party would take votes away from the Republicans; 2) Republicans did not want to sign because, due to the media slanting, they blamed Perot for Clinton winning the presidency in 1992; 3) most independents signed immediately; and 4) the main reason people signed the petition was that they thought the American people needed more viable choices when it came to electing a President."

I would add a few reasons why I think it was harder to gather signatures in 1996 than in 1992. First, in 1996, Perot, who got nearly 20 percent of the popular vote in 1992—a very threatening amount to the Republicans and Democrats—was locked out of the presidential debates by the two parties represented on the Commission on Presidential Debates, severely reducing his visibility to the voters. Second, reporters and the media trivialized Perot's candidacy and questioned his motives and even his sanity—and they haven't stopped since. Third, any political "outsider" who appeals to the public and has money will continue to be attacked by the major party members since an "outsider" is seen as a threat to the status quo and the entrenched political establishment.

In the mid-1990s, we the people and Reform Party members and supporters were fortunate to have a leader and presidential candidate with the money and the commitment to get eight million people to vote for Ross Perot in spite of the hurdles set up by the two established parties.

In 1996, it became clear to many of us that the signature collection process laws, like ballot access, needed to be streamlined and coordinated across the country by our elected officials in order to increase our choices for elected office and reduce the cost. The quandary is how to get those already elected under the existing, exclusionary system to make the changes that would open them up to more competition. We're still trying to solve that dilemma.

Chapter 8

The 1996 Reform Party Primary

In 1996, United We Stand America was continuing to have an impact, and the Committee to Establish the Reform Party participants were collecting signatures for ballot access in all fifty states. During that summer, the first Reform Party primary was about to take place.

Richard (Dick) Lamm

Mark Sturdevant, a California member of UWSA, heard Ross Perot say in 1996, "I have no intention of running. We're looking for George Washington II." Mark stated, "I took Ross at his word and called Dick Lamm [former governor of Colorado] to see if he would be interested in running. The reason I liked him was his willingness to take on 'third-rail issues' like social security reform and immigration reform. He was and still is an expert in both. His first question to me was 'Is Ross Perot going to run?' I told him what I repeatedly heard and the answer was no, I don't believe so. After many, many phone calls over a long period of time he said he would consider it."

According to Mark, "Perot continued to say he wouldn't run. Lamm said if I do this, will you support me? I gave him my word, of course I would. We had no other candidate coming up and he certainly was qualified. I had even called Dallas to make sure Perot wasn't going to run and were they interested in having the former Governor as a candidate. Russ Verney said yes and repeated the refrain 'we are looking for another candidate.' I proceeded with Lamm into the June [1996] California Reform Party Primary Nominating Convention hoping others would see what I saw and many did. However, so many had strong affection for Perot, as did I, it made it difficult to think of someone else carrying this reform banner. Imagine though, a presidential candidate supported by Ross Perot and the Reform Party. This candidate would have amazing potential. Lamm still had not committed to me or anyone that he was a candidate and was still waiting to see if Perot changed his mind."

Mark continued, "Finally, after long arduous talks and a visit to Colorado, it looked fairly certain we had George Washington II ready to go. Lamm made his Colorado announcement in early July; Lamm would be a candidate for the Reform Party nomination."

However, Mark said, "Traveling to San Jose to join up with his running mate Ed Zschau and a few of us he (Lamm) still wondered if Perot would run. We learned Ross was going to be on Larry King that evening and we were all watching the show together with over twenty television cameras and a number of reporters watching us. Then Perot said it, 'The people want me and I will run for the Reform Party nomination.' I cannot recall ever feeling so let down in my entire life. Here I had asked Lamm to run and repeatedly answered his question is Perot going to run with no after no after no. I had no choice at that point but to support Lamm to win. The rest is history."

Mark added a final note: "Despite our different paths and reasons for getting involved in the 'Perot movement,' I can still say this was a great moment in history that we can all be proud of and we owe it to Ross Perot and the people who got off their political couches and did something. We did make a difference.... Believe me, I am forever grateful to Ross Perot and his patriotism. It's just no fun running against a billionaire in his own party."

Jim Mangia, another volunteer and Perot supporter from California, had a different view of the Lamm situation. Jim said, "What was so disturbing was that we would be in a meeting with Lamm and his people where we would come to an agreement on a host of issues related to the primary, and then Lamm would literally walk out of the meeting into a barrage of press and television cameras, and charge that Perot was stacking the election in his favor and it wasn't a fair contest! It was disheartening."

Diane McKelvey from Michigan said, "I tried to be fair and open minded when Lamm came on the scene. I watched him on TV whenever he appeared. The first time I heard him I thought he sounded okay with the way he was presenting the issues. This was before Ross committed himself to the presidential race. However, the more I listened to Lamm, the more he didn't ring true and didn't seem dedicated. Perhaps it was the politician I saw in him."

Diane continued, "When Ross Perot threw his hat in the ring, it was at this point that Lamm began talking to the media about things not being fair. Perot had a mailing list and he didn't. Perot had money, and he didn't. Lamm also made a big deal about whether or not he would be first on the agenda to speak at the Valley Forge Reform Party Primary Announcement Convention. From the time Perot declared his candidacy, all Lamm did was whine. I guess he thought the nomination was going to be handed to him on a silver platter."

Regardless of each candidates' supporters' points of view, the Reform Party primary process was eventually established.

Primary process

Before Dick Lamm declared himself a Reform Party primary candidate for president, Mike Hicks, who helped establish the primary process, said, "It was decided that we would let anyone who signed a Reform Party petition or registered as a Reform Party member vote in the 1996 Presidential primary. This was an interesting twist, which helped address the problem that there were some states allowing registration, but some that would not. Also, some states would not allow petition collection processes to begin until after the primary dates.

"When Dick Lamm decided to enter the primary, the decision was made that we would let people call in and request ballots, as some of his supporters would not have opportunities to sign petitions or register. Some were opposed to signing petitions for Ross Perot, and some states required that we gain ballot access by placing Perot on the ballot as an independent individual."

Mike continued, "A team of Reform Party national leaders—Russ Verney, Mike Morris, the CFO, and myself were joined by Perot's personal advisors to determine a way to create a process that would be accurate, fair, auditable, and above reproach. The ... team was assigned the task of working out the technical process, and the others were there to be certain the process met the other criteria.... Ernst & Young [auditing professionals] were engaged to audit the process and validate the fairness."

Mike also pointed out, "Other 'firewall' rules were stipulated:

1. The vendors for the telephone, Internet, and mail balloting could not contact any Reform Party leaders [as most of us were Perot supporters] or other Perot friends or associates during the week that the voting took place. They could only communicate with the representatives from Ernst & Young.

2. Ernst & Young employees were prohibited from discussing preliminary vote counts or any other aspects of the voting process except to discuss the process with the vendors. This was very clearly defined in the agreement with Ernst & Young.

3. Processes were defined to deal with technical problems should they arise. As I was an obvious Perot supporter, I could not be involved in the problem resolution, so independent process and IT [Information Technology] resources were defined if they were needed. There were no technical problems with the vote collection process, so this plan was not used.

4. A process for validating, counting, and storing the printed ballots [in a lock box] was agreed upon with the American Caging company. It was agreed that they would hold the ballots for audit, but that no one else would ever see the ballots so we could keep the votes of the members private.

5. A similar process was created with Connexion.com. The data records would identify the PIN number of the voters, but not their names. This would allow a fair audit without revealing the votes of the members.

6. Ernst & Young created the file of PIN numbers to provide to the company that printed the ballots. This prohibited stuffing of the ballot boxes by the RPUSA [Reform Party USA] staff—something that would have been possible if we had created the PIN list ourselves.

7. All returned ballots were delivered to Ernst & Young rather than Perot Systems. Prior to their being delivered to Ernst & Young, the ballots were drilled through to be certain they would never be counted.

8. Ernst & Young created a file of returned ballot PIN numbers and validated so that none of these PIN numbers were used for voting.

9. All addresses for all ballots were validated against valid address files obtained from United States Postal Service. Initial thoughts were not to send any without valid addresses, but the decision was later made to mail to all addresses. The USPS has been known to make mistakes."

Once these precautions were instituted, Mike said, "It was decided that people would be allowed to vote by mail, by phone, or by Internet. We engaged Antonio Salerno, owner of Connexion.com, to deliver the Internet piece.... Antonio worked with a web development firm to create the voting site. It was determined that we would not place our member databases on line, but would allow anyone to go through the process, rejecting any non-valid votes. To do this, we had to generate 17-digit PIN numbers, place those on ballots, and mail the ballots to the members. Once they received the ballots, they could a) mark the ballot and mail it back, b) call a telephone number and vote electronically, or c) go to the Internet site and vote on line. This was revolutionary in the world of voting. No one had created a three-channel national primary election.

"We engaged American Caging of Houston, Texas, to receive the paper ballots and provide tallies. They utilized an electronic scanning system to provide 'quick counts' to Ernst & Young, then counted each ballot by hand to guarantee accuracy."

According to Mike, similar processes were used in the telephone-based capture of votes.

Mike also enjoyed "the broadcast of the primary conventions ([this is a quote from Mike.] held in Long Beach, California, and Valley Forge, Pennsylvania) via the Internet—another RPUSA first.... At the time, there was no such thing as consumer broadband or DSL. We had dedicated communication lines run into the convention sites so the AudioNet guys could set up their workstations, routers, cameras, etc., to broadcast. Each site cost about $50,000 to broadcast, using $30,000 worth of hardware."

In retrospect, Mike's experience with the media during the primary process was both disturbing and amusing. He said, "At the end of the first of the two RPUSA conventions [at Long Beach first in June, and later in August at Valley Forge], the voting channels were turned on and people began voting. The following day, Rush Limbaugh and Gordon Liddy began talking on their radio programs about how they could make up numbers and vote, and how they could vote as many times as they wanted. We didn't consider the 'moron factor' that these guys would think their votes were counting. I called their broadcast headquarters and insisted to each that they put me on with the hosts to explain how the voting system worked. Although they did allow me to explain how we would validate the votes, they were both very negative, forcing the conversation back to every bogus rumor about Perot when given the chance."

1996 Reform Party Presidential Nominating and Announcement Conventions

As Mike Hicks said, there were two conventions. According to Russell Verney, the former chairman of the Reform Party, "One was the nomination convention (Long Beach in June 1996) which opened the balloting and the other (Valley Forge in August 1996) was the announcement of the outcome of the balloting."

Judy Duffy was the coordinator for the Reform Party Presidential Nominating Convention in Long Beach, California. She said, "Prior to the event there were tables where attendees would come to sign in and get their primary ballots. I had a group of people who did a Civil War reenactment along with people giving famous speeches roaming around the staging area. At the far outside was the 'free speech' area. There were people speaking for Immigration Reform and other issues too numerous to mention. There was a small band playing when the people entered the building where the convention was held. No signs, etc., but of course there were banners under coats in the summer! There were to be no candidate flyer handouts, but candidate volunteers handed out cases of candidate flyers as people entered the convention center." She continued, "This was a TV event and required entertainment, a major media center, and volunteer coordination."

The Reform Party Presidential Primary Announcement Convention took place in August 1996 in Valley Forge, Pennsylvania. I attended that Valley Forge convention covered with campaign finance reform buttons. A couple came dressed as Uncle Sam and his wife, Mrs. Sam! Banners supporting the primary nominees were hung all over the convention site. There was entertainment and, of course, numerous speeches. I had a wonderful time.

Jim Mangia, from California, attended both conventions and said, "I thought they were tremendous events."

Primary results

Jim Mangia voted for Perot. He explains, "I supported Perot because I believed that he best represented the diverse views of the Reform Party and the collective agreement that this would be a party of reform that supported political reform and fiscal responsibility, and would not become involved in 'hot-button' social issues. Perot led that 'reform' perspective. In my opinion Lamm ... wanted to take the party in a different more ideological direction."

Most Reform Party members agreed with Jim. Ross Perot overwhelmingly won the primary.

Chapter 9

The 1996 Presidential
Campaign and Election

In the 1996 presidential election, Ross Perot's votes accounted for over 8 percent of those cast by American voters. *Why did almost twenty million people vote for Ross Perot in 1992, but only eight million vote for Ross Perot in 1996?*

In the opinion of Jim Mangia, "I think basically, Perot's numbers dropped in 1996 because he was excluded from the presidential debates. This may sound extreme, but there seemed to be a media conspiracy to prevent coverage of the Perot effort. This seemed astounding to me given he had received 19 million votes [for president] in 1992 in an unprecedented revolt at the polls by the American people. The political establishment did everything they could to prevent that from happening again—it was shocking. The fact is in 1992 before Perot entered the [presidential] debates, he was showing at roughly the same numbers as he was in 1996 before the debates. So that single effort [of keeping Perot out of the debates] had a major impact on his vote totals in 1996.

Jim said, "Also, I think that a lot of voters may have been more inclined to support Perot as an independent rather than a third-party candidate, but we'll never know whether this was the case, since the same conditions did not exist in 1992 and 1996."

Jim continued, "Perot was kept out of the debates to perpetuate the two-party monopoly and prevent the development of a major third party. If Perot had gotten 19 million votes as a Reform Party candidate [vs. as an independent candidate] it would have had an even more profound impact on the American political process and could have destroyed the two-party system. Given how well Perot had done in the 1992 debates, the Democratic and Republican parties could not allow a repeat when there was a possibility of building significant infrastructure on the ground through a third party as a result."

Asked that same question, Mike Hicks said Ross Perot's numbers dropped in the 1996 election because of "exclusion from the debates. Character assassination by the Sunday morning programs, Limbaugh, Liddy, etc." He believes Ross Perot was kept out of the debates because "he was a threat to the established political forces."

When asked how exclusion of alternative party candidates from the presidential debates can be prevented in the future, Jim Mangia said, "In 2000, they also kept Ralph Nader out of the debates, so keeping Perot out in 1996 was clearly a precedent-setting action. There must be objective criteria up-front in order to qualify. In 1996 and 2000 they said a third party or independent candidate had to be registering 15 percent in the polls to be included. *Whose polls?* [Emphasis mine.] And the fact that Perot had received almost 20 percent of the vote in the previous election wasn't a factor? It was a travesty, and unless they take the management of the debates out of the hands of the Debate Commission [which is a private group exclusively run by former Republican and Democratic Party officials] and put it into the hands of a truly independent commission with objective criteria—you'll never have real debates. Given that it is essentially inaccessible to all candidates and increasingly meaningless, viewership continues to drop."

Mike's answer to the aforementioned debate question was, "I do not believe it [exclusion from the presidential debates of alternative party and independent presidential candidates] can be prevented. As George Wallace said, 'There's not a dime's worth of difference between a Republican and a Democrat.' They know it. We know it. Everyone seems to be in denial that it's them against the citizens."

Donna Donovan, a volunteer from Connecticut and Reform Party national communications chair, agreed with both Jim Mangia and Mike Hicks. In fact, in the November 1997 Reform Party National Convention magazine *The Citizen*, which was given to all convention attendees, Donna gave a concrete example of the two major parties' fear of an alternative party through exclusion from the presidential debates, as well as media bias and media blackout.

In 1997 Donna wrote, "It was just a little more than a year ago. I remember the date ... October 6 ... because it's my birth date. And I'll never forget the events of that day which led me to a place I never thought I'd be, and to a conclusion I didn't want to draw.

"When Ross Perot was excluded from the Presidential Debates his Connecticut supporters decided to stage a 'Demonstration for Democracy' in Hartford, the state capital, while one of the three debates was taking place on October 6, [1996]. Our goal was to create a big enough media event to bring attention to the stranglehold that the two major parties and their accomplice, the bipartisan Debate Commission, maintained on the debates, which virtually guaranteed that a third-party candidate could not win.

"We planned to march through the city to a park a block away from Bushnell Theater where the debate was taking place. We circulated flyers, promoted the event on radio talk shows, and called our activists, asking them to join us in our peaceful torchlight march. And we notified the media, local, state and national, about our demonstration and our message.

"That night, nearly 700 people, carrying signs, banners and American flags, converged on the park, where we encountered police, who immediately herded us into a 'corral' constructed of a snow fence in the center of the park. As we moved into the area in peaceful fashion, shocked at how we'd been 'greeted,' a phalanx of black vans pulled up to the barricaded street next to the park, and hordes of state police emerged, armed and in full riot gear. They marched in military formation, eventually surrounding us completely. They stood, arms on hips, facing us about 10 feet outside the fence.

"Police officers on horseback formed another ring around the riot squad. Then unbelievably, National Guard forces arrived with tanks, and took their places on the streets around the park.

"You could hear a flag wave in the soft evening breeze. The demonstrators— all 700 of us—were silent ... dead silent. As we stared at our 'protectors,' and the reality of their presence and our virtual imprisonment sunk in, a collective instinct took over. As one mind, we began to recite, 'I pledge allegiance, to the flag....' Then we sang 'The Star-Spangled Banner' and every other patriotic song we could think of. Some people wept, as did a Ukrainian gentleman who told me he never thought he would see this type of oppression again after leaving his homeland.

"A few newspaper reporters found their way into our corral, as did one radio reporter with a tape recorder. A freelance cameraman was shooting footage for C-SPAN, but days later we were told that it was 'too dark' to use.

"And what about the rest of the media ... the hundreds of other reporters and cameramen and others who were in Hartford that night but not in the theater where the debate was taking place? We later heard from some that police and other security told them there was no one in the park, and since the direct-access streets were closed off, they assumed it was true.

"In all, few media representatives found us—and even fewer newspapers, TV and radio stations carried anything about our demonstration. They carried pictures and stories about tiny, obscure fringe groups who were carrying placards and making noise in other places around the city. But no one seemed to think that it was news that 700 people who came to demonstrate peacefully for the rights of Ross Perot and other third-party candidates were surrounded and under siege in the park that night.

"I still get a chill each time I think of that October 6 ... not so much because of the fences and the armed guards and the armored tanks. I had spent a number of years working in the media myself, and four years as a communications volunteer in the Perot campaign and United We Stand America. But I never believed that the media ever deliberately chose not to report on significant news. Now, I had no choice but to believe it. The evidence had stared me right in the face."

Meanwhile, Perot's press secretary, Sharon Holman, and others in the Dallas campaign office had been poring over data they had collected about the financing of the Commission on Presidential Debates, and had uncovered some very interesting information about the identity of the commission's key benefactors. As she detailed in the following press release dated September 26, 1996, Holman exposed the fact that ten of the fifteen major corporations that funded the Commission on Presidential Debates were also members of USA*NAFTA—the prime lobbying group for the North American Free Trade Agreement. And who was NAFTA's most visible and vocal opponent? Ross Perot.

To: Donna Donovan

From: Perot 96,
9–27–96 3:43pm

FOR IMMEDIATE RELEASE—September 26, 1996 CONTACT: Sharon Holman (972) 450–8803

Pro-NAFTA Corporations Bankrolled Debate Commission and Its Members

DALLAS (Sept. 26)—Why won't the voters be hearing from Ross Perot in this year's presidential debates? Perhaps because the corporations bank-rolling the bipartisan Commission on Presidential Debates (CPD) have heard quite enough from the populist Texan already.

Incomplete financial records released by the debate commission indicate 15 major corporations have provided much of the panel's funding. According to the Institute for Policy Studies, ten of the 15 were also members of USA*NAFTA, the lobbying consortium that pushed for congressional approval of the North American Free Trade Agreement in 1993. Perot was NAFTA's most visible and voluble opponent that year.

Three of the commission's corporate patrons—AT&T, General Motors, and 3M— served as USA*NAFTA "captains" in 13 states.

The financial ties that bind do not stop there. The corporate PACs of the 15 CPD sponsors also gave $106.148 in campaign contributions over the last decade to the four Commission members who have served in Congress.

The link could be vital to Perot's strategy as he mounts a legal challenge to the CPD decision that excluded him from the debates. "Corporate expenditures in elections are banned by law," explains American University law school dean Jamin Raskin. "*Corporations can fund debates, as long as they are staged in a non-partisan and objective manner. Plainly, the CPD has not operated that way. This money is simply illegal campaign contributions."

All ten of the CPD's members are politically well-connected Republicans or Democrats. Co-chairman Paul Kirk once chaired the Democratic National Committee and is now a registered lobbyist. The other co-chair, Frank Fahrenkopf, is a former chief of the Republican National Committee; his firm represents the gambling industry on Capitol Hill.

"We've known the debate commission was a shill for the two established political parties all along," commented Perot running mate Pat Choate during a television interview this afternoon in Seattle. "Now we know it is a paid lackey for the NAFTA lobby as well."

Other USA*NAFTA corporations that have funded the CPD include tobacco giant Phillip Morris, Dow Chemical, Ford, Upjohn (pharmaceuticals), Prudential Insurance, Kellogg and Hallmark Cards. Other corporate CPD sponsors include Brown & Williamson Tobacco, J.P. Morgan, ARCO, Dunn & Bradstreet and United Food.

The CPD congressional members who have received money from these corporations via their PACs: ex-Sen. Jack Danforth (R-MO) $38,250-.Sen. Paul Coverdell (D-GA) $31,000 . Rep. Barbara Vucanovich (R-NV) $23,100-; and Rep. John Lewis (D-GA) $13.798.

Unfortunately, given the media's bent for ignoring news from the Perot campaign, these facts didn't receive much coverage, and nothing changed.

Four years later, on October 3, 2000, Ralph Nader ran into similar problems with the Commission on Presidential Debates. He had a ticket issued by the University of Massachusetts to get into The Lipke Auditorium, "which was reserved for people to watch the debate on closed circuit television." Ralph Nader continued, "We were met by a man, escorted by a state trooper and two other men in police uniforms, claimed to be representing the Commission on Presidential Debates. He said he had been instructed by the Commission that regardless of whether I had a ticket, I was not welcome and would have to leave.... State Trooper Sergeant McPhail stepped forward and stated that if I did not leave, he would have to arrest me.... The trooper became more impatient ... and the sergeant said, 'Mr. Nader, is it your intention to be arrested here?' My immediate thought was: What the hell? In the United States of America, I have a ticket to a public function at a public university, and without any cause or disruption, the authorities are throwing me out of the place. A private corporate power is using the state's police for its partisan political ends. Sounds like a definition of the corporate state. See you in court, man.'" (Nader 2002, 220–1).

Ralph Nader asked, "How did this cancer in our democracy get started? How did it become an instrument of the two major parties, which have received millions in taxpayer dollars, to assure that only their candidates reach tens of millions of voters, not any of their challengers, even those whose participation is wanted by a majority of Americans polled?" (ibid., 223).

Ralph Nader gives five ingredients in the recipe for success to exclude all but the two major political party candidates from the presidential debates. "First, make sure that the major elements of the two [major] parties are in on the deal.... Second, connect with the corporate money to fund your operation.... Third, keep competitors off the debates under the guise of objective criteria.... In 1996, Perot, having garnered nineteen million votes four years earlier, was just under 10 percent in the polls and therefore was deemed not to have a chance. So he was cut off at the pass.... Fourth, secure the full and exclusive cooperation of the television networks.... Fifth, make sure you cover your rear with the Federal Election Commission [which is made up of Democrats and Republicans]" (ibid., 225–9).

All of the factors listed by Jim Mangia, Mike Hicks, Donna Donovan, and Ralph Nader combined keep alternative party candidates and independents out of the presidential debates. Diane McKelvey summed it up when she said, "Perot's performance in the 1992 debates was a lesson learned by the Democrats and Republicans. The major parties lived in a glass house and Perot had the stones. Never would they leave themselves open to this again." The exclusion from presidential debates reduced the visibility of non-major-party candidates and reduced their chances of being heard by the public.

Indirect or direct control of information about candidates running for office by corporations, the major political party candidates, the Commission on Presidential Debates, the Federal election commission, and the media plays a major role in determining who can win an election.

Can this control be moderated? Can information about all candidates running for office and their issue views be made available through every media outlet?

The only long-term solution to this problem of limited candidate information will come from you, the American voter. You can demand that all candidates be heard. Using the tools listed later in this book—writing letters to the editor, writing articles, working with lobbying groups, using the courts—will help change the rules made by those who want to retain and/ or increase their power.

In 1996, after the lessons of that election, the activist supporters of Ross Perot decided to continue to use one of the tools of vigilance—organizing and building an alternative political party, the Reform Party, to provide a voice for millions of unheard Americans.

Chapter 10

Building the Reform Party

Now that the 1996 presidential election was over, it was time for CERP (the Committee to Establish the Reform Party) members to build a structural foundation. The hard work of writing the national party rules, setting up a national party issues platform, and electing national party leaders began in January 1997 at the Reform Party Organizing Meeting in Nashville, Tennessee.

The party's formation

However, before even then and right after the 1996 election, the Reform Party state organizations began to solidify. For example, in New Jersey, a small group of "active campaign volunteers" began the process of building the New Jersey Reform Party (NJRP) foundation. Heading the initial group was Norris Clark, who had led the 1996 Perot presidential campaign in New Jersey. Bev Kidder, Ceil Sybrandy, Vince LoCascio, and I were the volunteer members. This group became the first NJRP Board of Trustees.

We set up the initial rules and regulations of the Reform Party organization (Reform Party of New Jersey, RPNJ) and incorporated as a nonprofit corporation on December 6, 1996, as required by the laws in New Jersey. Becoming a recognized political party in New Jersey was (and still is) cumbersome, to say the least. In New Jersey, qualification as a party can only be achieved by running candidates in more than one election. So our short-term solution in 1996 was to organize as a nonprofit business.

Then on January 3, 1997, the RPNJ Board of Trustees sent out an invitation to attend the first official RPNJ meeting. We advertised for an open-to-the-public political party meeting to be held on January 14, 1997. This meeting allowed us to give the supporters an update on Reform Party happenings, both nationally and in New Jersey. It also allowed for input from those who had voted for Ross Perot and/ or supported our platform. This meeting provided us with the support and information we needed at the upcoming national organizing meeting in Nashville, Tennessee.

Another state, Oklahoma, was also preparing for the January 1997 meeting in Tennessee. The Reform Party of Oklahoma, under the leadership of Dale Welch Barlow, conducted a "Reform Party Survey for State Chairs." In a follow-up report dated January 25, 1997, Dale Welch Barlow included her four-page commentary on the survey. Dale said, "[This report was] sent to all state chairs and selected volunteers around the country whose input we felt might be especially helpful."

She continued, "As recently as two days ago, copies of the survey were still being returned to us and we were still posting entries into our computer.... As a result, some of this data still remain to be analyzed ... survey results indicate we have many highly motivated volunteers in almost every state with not only top-of-the-line computer and Internet skills, but with writing skills, editing and publishing skills, marketing and advertising experience and a variety of other talents."

As Dale pointed out, "Our party is a young party and at the time of the [1996 presidential] election we were only a few months old in most states. Thus only half of the respondents had established offices or headquarters prior to the election." This survey clearly indicates that the Reform Party was still in the infant stages.

In late 1996, at the same time the Reform Party state groups were beginning to organize and build membership, another alternative party was considering folding its membership into the newly created Reform Party. This organization was called the Patriot Party.

The Patriot Party published a newsletter called *Patriot News*. In the "Special 1996 year-end Double Issue" of this newsletter, edited by Jacqueline Salit, were the following words: "Having achieved its first goal of inducing Ross Perot and his supporters to join the third party movement, the National Patriot Party immediately focused its attention on how to relate to Perot and the Reform effort."

It should be noted that members of fourteen UWSA state groups, at the 1995 UWSA national conference in Dallas, had petitioned the UWSA national organization to segue into an alternative party. Since the fall of 1994, this move to a political party had been building within UWSA.

The article in the *Patriot News* continued, "The California Patriot Party immediately began its participation in a joint effort to establish the California Reform Party as a ballot status group. Following the successful California effort, Patriot/Reform partnerships developed along varied lines in numerous states."

Eventually, the Patriot Party folded into the Reform Party, bringing in new members including Jim Mangia of California and Lenora Fulani of New York. These two people from the same political party represented different points of view. In the future, both were to have a major impact on the direction taken by the Reform Party.

However, before this merger of the Patriot Party and Reform Party could be completed, the underlying party structure had to be built. CERP members set up the credentialing process, proposed agenda, and meeting logistics (time, transportation, and accommodations). The actual construction began with the initial organizing meeting, led by CERP, on January 25 and 26, 1997.

Nashville Conference

On December 23, 1996, a notice was sent to "state Reform Party leaders." The letter said, "There will be a meeting of the state Reform Party leaders on January 25 and 26, 1997 in Nashville, Tennessee." The notice statement also included the following: "The meeting will begin at 9:00 a.m. and will be conducted by the representatives from states where there is no disagreement about the appropriate representative. The first order of business will be for these uncontested state representatives to decide each of the contested state representative cases." This meeting, like many others to follow, opened with a problem to solve.

Once the credentialing process ended, presentations were made by Ross Perot, his 1996 running mate Pat Choate, and a panel of people addressing "the future impact of the Reform Party on our traditional two-party political system." Then, attendees moved to breakout sessions (committee meetings) to discuss party development, fundraising, issues/platform, and communications.

As items on the agenda were being addressed in the meeting hall, outside in the corridors and in private rooms, the darker side of politics was rearing its head. People were lobbying for their choices of interim officers. Some people were cutting deals to support candidates from various groups. Promises were made, some of which were conveniently forgotten back in the meeting hall.

In addition, you could hear people discussing the issues/platform, along with the content of the other committees' meetings that day. Notice in the following material (figure 10.1) how similar these problem descriptions and proposed solutions are to issues discussions in 2007.

This was not a quiet group of people. Representatives came from all over the country. And, many of the ideas presented were influenced by the home turf of the presenters. For example, corrupt government was an issue for people from New Jersey and Illinois. Interest in the illegal immigration issue was high for people from states bordering Mexico, including Arizona, New Mexico, and California. Delaware also chimed in on the immigration question, as you can see in figure 10.2.

"vote your conscience"

THE REFORM PARTY OF DELAWARE

■■■■■■■■■■■■■■■■■■■■■■■■■■■■■■■■■

Telephone 328-1233/6794fax 832-0215/2377fax 628-0133ph&fax 678-1462 email Frank 5963 @ aol.com

IMMIGRATION

TO BE LIMITED TO ADMITTING NO MORE THEN 100,000 LEGAL
IMMIGRANTS INTO THE UNITED STATES PER YEAR. THAT NO ILLEGAL
IMMIGRANTS SHALL BE ADMITTED INTO THIS COUNTRY UNDER ANY
CIRCUMSTANCES WHATSOEVER. THE ADMISSION OF 100,000 IMMIGRANTS
PER YEAR REFERS TO THE NUMBER OF INDIVIDUALS THAT CAN BE
SUPPORTED WITHOUT DEGRADING THE NATURAL, CULTURAL AND
SOCIAL ENVIRONMENT. I.E. WITHOUT REDUCING THE ABILITY OF THE
ENVIRONMENT TO SUSTAIN THE DESIRED QUALITY OF LIFE OVER THE
LONG TERM.

THAT THE CONCENTRATION CAMPS (PRISONS) HOLDING ILLEGAL ALIENS
BE CLOSED DOWN AND THE ILLEGAL ALIENS BE EXPELLED TO THEIR
NATIVE COUNTRY.

THE PRESENT OBJECTIVE OF IMMIGRATION IS TO FLOOD THE COUNTRY
WITH IMMIGRANTS TO KEEP WAGES LOW AND UNION BUSTING, WHICH IS
NO ADVANTAGE TO ANY CITIZEN OF THE UNITED STATES. IT IS ONLY
CREATING A MASSIVE EXPENSE OF $100 BILLIONPER YEAR OF TAXPAYERS
MONEY, BY INTEGRATION INTO OUR SOCIAL SYSTEMS, I.E; SOCIAL
SECURITY, MEDICARE, MEDICAID, HOUSING, PRISONS AND WELFARE.

ROBERT HOLLINGSWORTH
VICE-CHAIRMAN
REFORM PARTY OF DELAWARE

Page 1 Deleware Reform Party Position Paper on Wages and Immigration

Also, a group in Delaware called Seniors Against Federal Extravagance (SAFE) sent in the following material that addresses the national debt and the federal entitlement programs:

December 1996

SAFE: ADVANCING OUR AGENDA

SAFE is an advocacy group for the next generations. We want to minimize the unfairness of the huge federal debt to our children and grandchildren. We recognize the danger of a financial crisis unless government spending is cut sooner and cut more than the politicians are even discussing. We believe it is necessary to give up something now to avoid giving up much more later. In contrast to other senior organizations, we do not want to maximize our gains at the expense of younger taxpayers. We are willing to give up some of our entitlements if federal government spending is decreased so that the debt can be paid.

To counter the dangerous effects of skyrocketing entitlements, we advocate the institution of Individual Medical Accounts and substitution of private savings for Social Security. We recognize that current retirees must be paid the Social Security they have counted on, and that a transition to private saving will require some sacrifice.

Our approach will be to use the strength of our organization and the strength of our ideas in as intelligent a way as we can to advance our agenda. We'll use education, publicity, and persuasion. We'll try to influence individuals and organizations rather than opposing them.

We believe the key to solving the debt problem and averting a financial crisis is to decrease the dollars spent from one year to the next. We will promote elimination or cut-back of specific government programs. This will of course be controversial. Consequently, we will seek consensus among SAFE members before proposing specific cuts.

Seniors Against Federal Extravagance—Bill Morris

SENIORS SHOULD HELP SOLVE ENTITLEMENT PROBLEM

We senior citizens are very interested in the well-being of our children and grandchildren. Most of us are willing to make sacrifices if needed to help and protect them. In that spirit, it is urgent that we help press the federal government to cut spending and to privatize Medicare and Social Security as soon as possible. Why is this necessary?

When the baby boom generation retires after 2010, there will be only two workers per retiree. Without changes, tax rates would have to be about 80%. This is obviously unacceptable, so changes will be made. If the government continues to postpone the required changes, our children can expect large cuts in entitlements, our grandchildren can expect large tax increases, and both generations could face a financial crisis. The needed adjustments will be much more moderate if they are made soon. Let us consider the federal debt, Medicare, and Social Security.

Because of government irresponsibility, the federal debt [in 1996] approaches $20,000 per citizen. This is obviously unfair to our children and grandchildren. There is talk about balancing the federal budget in 2002, two years after the present administration. However, that would not solve the problem of skyrocketing entitlements when the baby boom generation retires. Lawrence Lindsay, a Governor of the Federal Reserve Board said "Neither proposal for a balanced budget by 2002 goes far enough to prevent a financial crisis later" (News Journal 2–2-96). Out of fairness to our children and grandchildren and out of prudence to prepare for baby boomer retirements and unpredictable future events, we need to balance the budget and start paying off the debt before 2002.

Direct and indirect taxes take almost half of our income, so higher taxes are unacceptable. Congress should focus their attention on cutting spending and obtaining budget surpluses well before 2002. Here are just a few suggestions: Eliminate corporate welfare, estimated to be over $75 billion per year. Streamline welfare administration that now uses 70% of welfare funds. Stop federal payments to the states. Every dollar going to a state is another dollar added to the debt. Individual states can compensate by getting their spending under control.

Cut government regulations to help the economy, thereby moving welfare recipients to the tax rolls. Start selling government assets with all proceeds going to retire the debt. This of course would decrease government spending on interest.

Health care costs are high because of the low incentive to control cost when Medicare or company health insurance pays most of the cost. Health insurance is tax deductible for employers. If employees were given the same tax treatment, employers could purchase catastrophic insurance with part of the health care funds and deposit the remainder in a Medical Savings Account for each employee. When using their own money, consumers would spend prudently and health care cost would come down. In addition, a decrease in paper shuffling would help cut the cost.

Privatization of Social Security is working well in Chile and elsewhere. By investing in stocks and bonds, workers can obtain greater income than from Social Security. The government is considering this, but the change needs to be made soon so that the baby boomers can accumulate enough in their private retirement accounts to cut down the huge entitlement tax after 2010. The problem is to pay the current retirees and put money in private accounts at the same time.

One source of the needed funds could be elimination of payments to the Social Security "Trust Fund" now used to mask the federal deficit. In addition, by accepting a Social Security means test, we senior citizens could provide more than $100 billion yearly for private accounts. Privatization would help solve the baby boom entitlement problem and minimize generational conflict between our children and grandchildren.

We seniors should do right by our children and grandchildren. Rather than leaving a mess for them to clean up, we should start cleaning it up now. We need to show our willingness to accept some discomfort now, to spare our children and grandchildren much greater discomfort later. An organization with these goals was formed in Delaware last year (1995).

The preceding is just one group's perspective on our country's economic problems.

However, even with the Reform Party's diversity across many issues, we were able to approve interim party rules and a national organizing team that included: Russell Verney, as interim chairman of the Reform Party National Organizing Committee; Dale Welch Barlow, as interim vice chair; Jim Mangia, as interim secretary; and Carl Owenby of Florida, as interim treasurer.

The party begins

After the January 1997 Nashville organizing meeting, we began the tedious work of writing the rules, building membership in the party, communicating with the public as well as within the party ranks, and setting up the platform upon which our candidates would run.

De Clapsadle and I worked together with a large team to organize the issues and write the Reform Party platform. States represented at the Nashville Issues Committee meeting included Washington, Ohio, Massachusetts, Colorado, Idaho, South Carolina, Alabama, Illinois, Kentucky, North Carolina, New Jersey, Michigan, Texas, Maryland, New Mexico, Virginia, Indiana, Oregon, Utah, Missouri, and California.

Unlike the major political parties today, our issues defined who we were and what we believed in. Although this group was founded around one person—Ross Perot—the issues are what really drove most of us to work hard in order to have our ideas impact this country.

Overseeing the various committees, including the Issues/Platform Committee, was Dale Welch Barlow of Oklahoma, the interim vice chair. One of her jobs was to keep the process moving toward completion by October 1997.

And Dale was definitely focused. I remember vividly one incident in particular. I was on the telephone with Dale when my husband appeared at the door of our home in the middle of the day. He looked terrible. Since the doctor had told us his brain tumor could be growing back, I was very alarmed. I said to Dale, "I have to hang up. My husband is home early and looks very sick." She replied, "Our discussion is more important. We have a deadline to meet. We need to finish talking about the platform and then you can hang up and take care of him." Needless to say, I hung up immediately—conversation over. Right or wrong, Dale's dedication was clear, and I was to experience more of her tenacity later that year.

The politics continue

Throughout 1997, De Clapsadle and I, with others on the Platform Committee, continued to work on the issues. At the same time, people were beginning to campaign for the upcoming state elections for delegates to the Reform Party National Committee and to the RP National Convention in Kansas City. In addition, decisions were being made on whom to support among those running for national chairman, vice chairman, secretary, and treasurer.

By September 1997, several people in New Jersey were suggesting I run for the vice chair slot. Everyone assumed Dale Welch Barlow would run for that position because she was already the interim vice chair. Another name that began to surface was Elizabeth Christman from Pennsylvania.

I had mixed feelings about running for the vice chairman position. It appeared to be focused on administrative duties, carrying out the directives given by the Executive Committee, and supporting the national chairman. In the past my interests had always centered on issues. However, I had run two businesses and enjoyed helping to establish start-up entities.

I waited until mid-October. Then, with the promised support of the New Jersey delegation, I decided to run for the office of RPUSA vice chairman.

In November 1997, at the Reform Party National Convention in Kansas City, these elections for party leaders were conducted. Russ Verney was elected chairman, Jim Mangia was elected secretary, and Mike Morris was elected treasurer. As expected, the vice chairman contest included three people—Dale Welch Barlow, Elizabeth Christman, and me.

The usual activities one would expect to take place at a political convention where elections occurred, did—campaigning, vote counting, and making deals about who to support for this 1997 election of new RPUSA officers. Once the speeches for vice chair were completed, the vote began. I found this experience stressful, to say the least. Some people enjoy campaigning and running for office—I'm not one of them. However, I do enjoy the work involved once the election is over. So, I went through the worst part to get to the best part.

This election involved a runoff because there were three candidates. The eventual outcome was worth the grief, since I was elected. Naturally, some people were happy and others were not. In fact, there was even some hysteria and screaming among supporters of the election losers. After the vote, a confrontation between me, the winner of the election, and the former interim vice chair took place back at the hotel. Let's just say it was a learning experience I'd rather not repeat. I was amazed at how high emotions ran. After all, no one gets paid, and the "power" is with the members, the National Committee, and the Executive Committee.

I was about to find out, over the next three years, just how ruthless and crazy people can become when politics of any kind is involved.

Chapter 11

1998: The Win?

In November 1998, a year after the Reform Party founding convention, lightning struck the political establishment. Jesse "The Body" Ventura, a Reform Party candidate, beat out the Republican and Democratic candidates, as well as seven others, to become governor of Minnesota. After winning the election, governor-elect Ventura declared, "We shocked the world."

How did this happen?

According to Dean Barkley, Jesse's campaign chairman, Jesse Ventura (née James George Janos) was recruited in 1996 during Dean's campaign for senator in Minnesota. Jesse was helping Dean and appeared with him in a Minnesota parade. Dean noticed more people were responding to Jesse than to him. Dean said to Jesse, "The wrong guy is running. You're running next." In January 1998, Jesse Ventura entered the race as the Reform Party candidate for governor of Minnesota.

This was not Jesse's first political office. He had been Mayor of Brooklyn Park, Minnesota, in the early 1990s. But, his longest-held job was as a professional wrestler with the WWF (now called the WWE).

As Paul Gray pointed out in the November 1999 issue of *Time* magazine with Jesse on the cover, "Here was a guy who had campaigned on a Harley.... He had been elected to a part-time job; most of the work was done by a paid manager, and the mayor's vote counted for no more than those of the six other members of the town council (56).

"Yet, the people responded well to Jesse," Paul Gray continued, "... the most potent weapon was his up-the-establishment attitude" (57).

In that same article, Gray states, "Democratic state representative Myron Orfield ruefully concedes Ventura's extra-political appeal: 'Jesse isn't just a former wrestler. He's a cultural phenomenon. He's connected to the modern vernacular of things here. He's with it'" (57).

In addition, according to Gray, "Ventura waged a campaign well within the mainstream of Minnesota political thinking. Outsiders view the state as a bastion of liberalism—witness Eugene McCarthy, vice presidents Humphrey and Mondale—but insiders disagree. Carleton College's [Steven] Schier said Minnesota 'is actually a quirky populist state. It gave 24 percent of its vote during the 1992 presidential election to Ross Perot. Ventura's fiscal conservatism of no tax increases, the return of all future state budget surpluses to taxpayers—struck a responsive chord. So did his moderate-to-libertarian views on keeping government from meddling unduly in private lives'" (57).

Finally, Jesse had been allowed to participate in the Minnesota gubernatorial debates. His opponents in the debates, Norm Coleman and Hubert Humphrey III, were boring, and that came through when the three candidates appeared together. Diane McKelvey, a Reform Party activist from Michigan, watched one of the debates on television. She said, "It was enjoyable watching his plain talk tongue-tie his opponents. For example, when a question was asked about a state issue to all three candidates, Ventura would bring forth a solution. The other two would put together a committee to study the problem. Sound familiar?"

As Schier from Minnesota's Carleton College pointed out about Ventura in the *Time* magazine article, "He's charismatic, he's warm, he's colorful. Coleman and Humphrey [the other candidates] were much more conventional politicians and produced a nice gray backdrop" (55).

Was it a win for the Reform Party?

This question may seem strange at first. However, as pointed out earlier, there were several factions within the Reform Party, and the Reform Party of Minnesota was in the forefront of one of them. In fact, right after Jesse's Minnesota win, I clearly remember a Reform Party activist saying to me, "Is it a win, or the beginning of the end of the Reform Party as we know it?"

The seeds of discontent in Minnesota actually go back to 1992–93. This was when the majority of activist Minnesota Perot supporters chose to build an alternative political party rather than join the issues group United We Stand America. Phil Madsen and Dean Barkley began that political party, called the Minnesota Independence Party. While most Reform Party members around the country were involved in politics almost as a necessary evil—as the way to get their issues on the table—the organizers in Minnesota seemed more comfortable with the political contest aspects of running an election.

The discontent between Minnesota members and other Reform Party activists grew at the January 1997 Nashville Committee to Establish the Reform Party Conference. As I mentioned earlier, backroom deals were brokered. Some held and some did not. According to Dean Barkley, there was an attempt to bring "peace to the warring factions." The two factions he referred to were those who had come to the Reform Party from UWSA—the issues organization, and those state delegates from the alternative political parties that were formed after 1992 in New York, Minnesota, Oregon, and Pennsylvania.

When the delegates elected Russ Verney (Texas), Dale Welch Barlow (Oklahoma), Jim Mangia (California), and Carl Owenby (Florida) as the interim leaders, delegates from the political parties in Minnesota and Oregon walked out. There were all kinds of rumors floating around that the deal among factions to support designated candidates fell apart.

The seeds of discontent had been planted in 1992 when the political reform movement was formed, without a national plan or strong state or local foundation. These seeds continued to grow all the way into January 1997, when the party delegates from Minnesota staged a walkout at the Nashville meeting to register their unhappiness with the results of the election.

When Jesse Ventura declared his candidacy the following year, 1998, the Minnesota Reform Party members were already distrustful of the National Reform Party and its leaders due to the meeting in Nashville. Jesse had clearly been told about these problems and obviously sided with his Minnesota supporters.

When candidate Jesse Ventura was invited to speak at the September 1998 Reform Party Convention in Atlanta, Georgia, his affirmative response took some time in coming. According to Dean Barkley, discussions were taking place with Reform Party leaders about the possibility of Perot helping Jesse to get a bridge loan for the campaign based on the public monies Ventura would get after the November election.

In an e-mail from Bob Maline, the treasurer of Jesse's campaign, Bob stated, "When we went to Atlanta, we had hoped Mr. Perot would be able to put us in touch with a bank that would loan us $310,000 so we could make use of public subsidy money that would not be paid to us until after the election. We met with Mr. Perot and his personal financial officer for about twenty minutes after he spoke to the convention on Saturday night. We reviewed the campaign finance law including the main constraint for him—the lending institution has to be chartered in Minnesota or through the federal government; it cannot be chartered with the state of Texas for example. Mr. Perot does not have extensive contacts in Minnesota and was not able to refer us to a financial institution that could help."

Mr. Maline continued, "Mr. Verney and Mr. Perot's personal financial officer called me three times the week following the convention. They had suggestions for financial institutions other than banks and savings and loans that I might use to obtain our loan. While their suggestions did not pan out, it did get me thinking of more off-beat methods ... this trail did keep our loan seeking alive for many days."

In fact, the Ventura campaign was able to get their bridge loan a week before the election from the Franklin National Bank in Minnesota.

Bob Maline also commented on the role of the National Reform Party in helping with money for Jesse Ventura's campaign. Bob said, "National Chair Russ Verney and convention organizer Mike Hicks told us they would arrange time to talk with Mr. Perot while we were at the convention. They accomplished this although the outcome, as described above was not as we would have wished.... I know they [the National Reform Party] are not allowed to make a direct contribution to the Jesse Ventura Committee. The Committee can only take contributions from individuals or associations registered with the state of Minnesota. ... Also, there are laws against the national party making a contribution to the state party with the explicit understanding that it will go to a particular candidate—such a practice is illegal ear-marking of a contribution."

Maline also said that he was given time at the Atlanta convention podium to tell people where to find him if they wanted to contribute to Jesse's campaign. He later reported that $20,650 came from members from other states that can be traced to their appearance at the convention. He said, "There were loans that came in from names and addresses given to me just outside the convention hall." In addition, they received "$12,000 in loans from party officers and long-time activists who were delegates to the convention."

Maline concluded, "My disappointment that we did not get all the financial support that we were hoping to receive from the national party leadership, official and unofficial, is balanced by the efforts put forth on our behalf by those same individuals and by the actual support we did receive from rank and file members in Minnesota and around the country. My own opinion—not shared by everyone on the campaign staff—is Jesse's trip to Atlanta was worth the time and expense."

In fact, National Reform Party leaders and members were invited to Jesse's inauguration in January 1999, and I—and the others who went—had a grand time, in spite of the sub-zero temperatures in Minnesota while we were there.

Unfortunately, the seeds of divisiveness continued to grow and spread, reaching a high in the springs and summers of 1999 and 2000.

Chapter 12

1999: Divisions Increase

Following Jesse Ventura's January 1999 inauguration as Minnesota governor, the focus of the Reform Party members turned to the coming election of new party leadership. Russ Verney decided not to run again for the office of Reform Party chairman, and I decided not to run for the vice chairman position.

At that point, I was approached by several people and asked to run for chairman. As I said before, running for office is not my favorite activity. And, in this case, I wasn't sure if the party—given the recent infighting and increasing divisions—could be united and strengthened. I decided to survey the members and speak with the leaders of the party before making a decision.

Ventura impacts again

In April 1999, I contacted Jesse Ventura's office to arrange for a meeting with him. I didn't hear back from anyone. I called again. Still no response. I heard that another member considering a run for party chairman, Tom McLaughlin of Pennsylvania, also had tried to arrange a meeting with Jesse and was ignored. Since I had spoken with Jesse at his inauguration, I was surprised by the silence.

Eventually, I found out that Jesse had already decided to support Jack Gargan of Florida for chairman. Dean Barkley, Jesse Ventura's former campaign chairman, told me that Jack had met with Jesse and the decision had been made. Interestingly, Dean had no idea that Jesse had ignored my request to meet with him. In fact, the meeting with Jack took place after I had requested a meeting with the governor. To this day, I have no specific information on why Governor Ventura chose to support Jack Gargan, nor why neither Tom nor I were even given time to talk with Jesse before he made that decision.

I continued talking with party leaders and members as I traveled to several states to introduce myself and answer questions. Also, many of us continued to try to convince Russ Verney to run again, but he was adamant that his decision was final. Russ seemed to be satisfied that Tom McLaughlin was running, but still continued to press me to run as well. Since Jesse was supporting Jack Gargan and Ross Perot had decided not to support or endorse anyone, I was not having an easy time making my decision on whether to run or not. However, I had concerns about the ability of either Jack Gargan or Tom McLaughlin to move the party forward, so I didn't feel I could vote for either one of them. That's what finally moved me to officially declare my candidacy.

Building and strengthening the party became my campaign message. I used yellow construction hard hats to symbolize my goals. I believed we needed to go back to basics, building the foundation of the Reform Party at the state and local levels. We needed to train the elected leaders, who held state and local positions; write and distribute a Reform Party "Playbook;" and strengthen two-way communication between state and national party leaders through a national newsletter.

But the underlying question that needed to be answered before even addressing these ideas was, could the various factions within the Reform Party be united to achieve these goals? At the time of the 1999 Reform Party Convention that was held in Dearborn, Michigan, from July 23 to July 25, there were three apparent divisions within the party.

First, there were the Perot activists who had started in 1992, later joined United We Stand America, and continued their involvement by joining the Reform Party. Many people had been added to this group since 1992, but other factions had co-opted some of these activists over time.

The second group was focused on Jesse Ventura and the Minnesota Reform Party led by Phil Madsen. With Jesse's successful campaign and election as governor of Minnesota, this group's impact on Reform Party members across the country had grown. This group had left the Perot-inspired reform movement when the focus turned away from campaigning and toward educating the public about national issues. Many of the members of this group wanted Perot's influence diminished and Jesse Ventura's role in the party increased. For example, most Reform Party members were against NAFTA, while Governor Ventura supported economic globalization.

The glue for the third faction was Lenora Fulani and the Independence Party of New York. This group tended to move to wherever the most power was concentrated at any given time. They came together after the 1992 Perot run for president as an independent, when their members decided to stay with a political party rather than join up with United We Stand America (UWSA). Eventually, they joined with Pennsylvania and became supporters of the Patriot Party. As mentioned before, the Patriot Party joined with the Reform Party in

January 1997 at the Nashville Reform Party formation conference. Tom McLaughlin had been an activist member in the Patriot Party.

These were the three strongest groups at the Dearborn Convention, and votes split along these lines.

On July 2, 1999, an Associated Press article appeared in the southern New Jersey newspaper, the *Courier-Post*, that presented an overview of the disagreements. Jesse Ventura and his faction endorsed Jack Gargan for chairman of the Reform Party, and supported moving the party headquarters from Dallas, Texas, to Cedar Keys, Florida, where Jack Gargan lived. Russ Verney and Perot supporters endorsed me for chairman. I stated, "I have a problem with building a party based on one individual, whether it is Ross Perot or Jesse Ventura." I wanted to concentrate on building a political party with strong foundations at the local and state levels, instead of just focusing on the national congressional and presidential candidates.

The Reform Party election

At the 1999 Reform Party Convention, the first vote taken for chairman resulted in placing Gargan first, Pat Benjamin second, and Tom McLaughlin third. Since we had a run-off rule, Tom's name was dropped and the second round of voting was between Gargan and me.

Tom's support base seemed to be the Fulani faction, and Tom urged everyone to vote his or her personal choice during the second vote rather than endorsing either remaining candidate. The day before, as we tried to forecast vote counts, I was told that the Fulani faction would go with the Perot supporters if Tom was removed from the contest. But that's not what eventually happened.

Once the second vote was taken, it was clear that the Jesse Ventura group won the day, as Jack Gargan was declared the new Reform Party chairman. His vice chair was Gerry Moan from New York. The secretary remained Jim Mangia, a Californian from the Fulani faction. And Ron Young, a Ventura/Gargan supporter from Iowa, became treasurer.

Diane McKelvey, expressing the view of many in the Perot activist group, was "totally upset." She continued, "A lot of backroom deals and political double crosses happened and the party fractured at this point. Ventura had turned out to be an embarrassment to the party when he endorsed Gargan."

But the people in the party were not ready to walk away.

According to the Reform Party Constitution, this group of newly elected officers was to take office officially on January 1, 2000. However, soon after the convention, Russ Verney tried to begin mending the rifts that had formed during the contentious campaign and convention by immediately including them in meetings and informing them of decisions being made that would impact the National Reform Party in 2000. These new officers also needed to begin to plan the 2000 Reform Party presidential nominating convention.

A fourth faction develops

At the same time the Dearborn Convention was taking place in July 1999, Republican Pat Buchanan was considering a leap from the Republicans to the Reform Party, with the intention of running for president in 2000 on the Reform Party ticket. Pat Choate, Ross Perot's 1996 running mate, was a strong supporter of Buchanan because of their shared anti-NAFTA views.

Once Pat Buchanan announced his intentions to run as a Reform Party candidate, his supporters began joining the Reform Party through the states and, in some cases, taking over the state parties.

Meanwhile, in the fall of 1999, Pat Buchanan and his sister Bay held a meeting with national and state Reform Party leaders at Pat Choate's apartment in Washington DC.

Detroit meeting

In September 1999, the same month that the Buchanan meeting took place, a request was made by an "outside" group to meet with Russ Verney (then–Reform Party chairman) and me in order to discuss the possibility of the Reform Party addressing a new issue. We flew to Detroit, Michigan, my hometown. We met with emissaries of Jesse Jackson, Al Sharpton, and Detroit church representatives to discuss the enforcement of the 14th Amendment—"equal protection under the law." The meeting was productive and very issues-focused. However, we were interrupted by a call giving us a heads-up that the November 1999 issue of *Playboy* magazine had just hit the stands, and in it there was an "outrageous" interview with Jesse Ventura.

In this lengthy, far-reaching, and candid interview, Ventura expressed personal opinions and made statements that raised eyebrows—and blood pressure. Among them:

"Organized religion is a sham and a crutch for weak-minded people who need strength in numbers. It tells people to go out and stick their noses in other people's business."

"It's good to be the king. The best thing [about being governor] is that there's no one who can tell me what to do."

"If I could be reincarnated as a fabric, I would come back as a 38 double-D bra."

Referring to former Minnesota first lady Barbara Carlson, who had told *Mirabella* magazine that Ventura "can dish it out but can't take it," Ventura said, "Consider the source.... This is a woman who struck the former governor with a frying pan.... She's also a woman who has had her stomach cut so she doesn't eat as much. What happened to willpower?"

In the same vein, Ventura said, "I love fat people. Every fat person says it's not their fault, that they have gland trouble. You know which gland? The saliva gland. They can't push away from the table."

Also, some more "outrageous" quotes from Ventura:

"If you buy the flag it's yours to burn."

"Drugs and prostitution, those shouldn't be imprisonment crimes."

"You're talking to an ex-Navy Seal here."

It would later come to light that though Ventura often referred to himself as a

member of that elite group, he had served on a Navy underwater demolition team
(UDT) and not as a Seal.

The *Playboy* debacle

The Ventura interview produced a deluge of phone calls to the national leadership from
Reform Party members all over the country. I personally heard from many members—all
very distressed about Jesse's damaging attitude and "outrageous ideas." Russ tried to call
Jesse immediately, while we were still in the meeting in Detroit. The first call produced no
response. When he called again, Russ was told he should fax in a request to talk with the
governor and that he might hear back from his office in about three months!

We held a telephone conference with the Reform Party Executive Committee and
agreed to send a letter to Jesse under Russ's signature.

That letter and Jesse Ventura's reply follow.

Russell J. Verney, Chairman   Jim Mangia, Secretary
Pat Benjamin, Vice Chair   Mike Morris, Treasurer

October 1, 1999

Governor Jesse Ventura
Statehouse
St. Paul, Minnesota

Via fax 651–296–0056
Dear Governor Ventura:

The members of the Reform Party are committed to restoring the public's faith and trust in our government. Above everything else the members of this party have tried to lead through example by setting high standards for ethics and integrity.

Your comments in the November 1999 Playboy article about religion, sexual assault, overweight people, drugs, prostitution, women's undergarments and many other subjects do not represent the values, principles or ethics upon which this party was built.

Members of the Reform Party from coast to coast are outraged about your comments. In just one interview you have managed to severely damage the credibility and integrity of thousands of Reform Party members.

You have brought shame to yourself and disgrace to the members of the Reform Party.

You can stop the cascading damage to the reputation of the members of the Reform Party by accepting personal responsibility for your actions and the attendant consequences.

For the good of the members, you should resign now from the Reform Party of the United States of America.

Sincerely,
Russell J. Verney

According to Russ, Jesse's reply was written on an official Office of the Governor card. The note said, "I have received your letter of October 1, 1999. Rest assured that your letter has been filed in the most appropriate place."

Pat Buchanan makes his move

During 1999, as the Ventura incident shows, the divisions within the Reform Party continued to deepen. Unfortunately, these divisions were only "helped along" by the meeting in Washington DC with Pat Buchanan and Pat Choate to discuss Buchanan's interest in becoming a Reform Party candidate for president.

There were ten Reform Party attendees, in addition to Pat and Bay Buchanan and Pat Choate. The members included Gerry Moan (New York), Donna Donovan (Connecticut), Diane and Alec McKelvey (Michigan), Dror and Cheryl Bar-Sadeh (North Carolina), Diane Goldman and her husband (Minnesota), and my husband Milton Benjamin and I (New Jersey).

Most of us at the meeting had concerns about Pat Buchanan's longtime focus on social issues, since members of the Reform Party had voted not to focus on social issue concerns and to mainly direct our attention toward political and economic reform. However, we did address the immigration issue, health care, and education. We ignored abortion, which Pat Buchanan discussed publicly quite often, and we suggested that he avoid this topic as much as possible. At the meeting he agreed to that request.

Other questions came up about his views on neo-Nazi and white supremacist supporters, anti-Semitism, and affirmative action. Since the questions were numerous, Pat Buchanan suggested he take down our questions and respond in writing soon after the meeting. I have his original responses, sent to me in a blue binder, which addressed all of the questions asked.

Diane McKelvey described her feelings about what transpired at that meeting: "In the fall of 1999 a small group from the Reform Party met with Buchanan in Washington DC at Pat Choate's condo. There was quite a bit of one-on-one conversation. Pat Buchanan was relaxed, easy going, and believable. One of my concerns was that he might be anti-Semitic. When one of the gathered groups posed some questions to him about this, Buchanan opted not to answer then but chose to write her a letter covering that issue. This bothered me a bit as I felt he had to think it over rather than be spontaneous. I left there not as sold on him as when I arrived but I still had a positive attitude toward him. However, the best part of the meeting was the lox and bagels that were served!"

She continued, "A few weeks later I was invited to attend a Buchanan meeting in Grand Rapids [Michigan]. Hardly anyone showed up. I had thought that with his following the room would be packed. There might have been a dozen of Buchanan's people there. The people I spoke with were far right one-issue, right-to-life individuals. That's all they cared about."

Finally, Diane says, "It took me about four weeks to come to the conclusion that Buchanan wasn't for real. The expression 'follow the money' kicked in and I began to believe he was not a serious candidate. In my opinion, the $13 million in federal matching funds is what he wanted."

I had one last conversation with Bay Buchanan in early January 2000. We began discussing where the 2000 Reform Party Convention should be held. We had different opinions. She hung up on me.

However, Lenora Fulani, an African American, and her New York contingent once again appeared to move to where the power resided—endorsing Pat Buchanan. This unusual partnership was announced before the media at the National Press Club in Washington DC, at which Fulani was named cochair of the Buchanan presidential campaign.

By then, many of us had decided against supporting Pat Buchanan and had begun looking at other options. While we discussed our choices, information began to trickle out about "deals" being made by Jack Gargan (RPUSA chairman) and Ron Young (RPUSA treasurer).

According to Pat Choate, contracts were being signed for work at the 2000 Reform Party convention. The vendors were "old line Democratic operatives and they [Gargan and Young] were putting the party in the hands of people we were running against [Democrats and Republicans]."

For example, in December 1999, before the newly elected officers took office, Young signed a contract with an entity called The Performance Group of Alexandria, Virginia, to "provide consulting and representative services in support, promotion and the advancement of initiatives of the Client [2000 Convention Committee of the Reform Party of the United States] ... in this role, the Consultant shall serve as liaison to ... organizations that are involved with the provision of services to the Convention Committee."

The signatories on this contract for The Performance Group were Daniel H. Murray, Robert J. Keefe, and Michael Foudy. Murray, an attorney, later joined Dutko Worldwide, a major lobbying firm with strong ties to the Democratic Party. Keefe is and was a registered foreign agent with TKC International, a Washington Lobbying firm. He is also a former executive director of the Democratic National Committee. And Foudy, a lawyer and talk show host, served on the board of the Democracy Foundation, a 501(c)3 organization founded by the former Democratic senator Mike Gravel.

Something had to be done to stop the sellout of the National Reform Party.

Chapter 13

2000: Changing of the Guard

In December 1999, several Reform Party activists began discussing how to deal with the problems being created by the new Jack Gargan leadership. As Pat Choate pointed out, the Gargan group was signing contracts and spending money before they actually assumed office. In addition, it became clear that Gargan was maneuvering to change the convention venue from Long Beach, California, to a location in Minnesota. Gargan's support for Minnesota appeared to be payback to the Ventura group for supporting him for National Reform Party (RPUSA) chairman.

The problem was that the 1999 Dearborn Convention delegates and National Committee had already voted to have Long Beach as the location. This had been a democratically chosen location and the existing Executive Committee believed the National Committee and delegates were the only ones who could make a change—not the yet-to-be inaugurated RPUSA chairman.

The national party structure and duties were very clear. RPUSA National Convention delegates had the final vote on all national party matters. When the convention was not in session, the National Committee members ran the party. The Executive Committee represented the party when the National Committee was not in session. The Executive Committee included the RPUSA chairman, vice chairman, secretary, and treasurer—all elected by the delegates at an RPUSA National Convention. Other members on the Executive Committee included the team leaders for communications, party building, etc. Therefore, the daily running of the party and the planning of conventions, as determined by the preceding convention delegates, were carried out by members of the Executive Committee.

An Associated Press article which appeared on December 29, 1999, in the *Philadelphia Inquirer* summed up the differences as "squabbles." Gargan called the opposition a small group of "yappers from only 15 states." And the Minnesota state party tried to get an injunction against the national party in order to stop them from holding the Reform Party 2000 Nomination Convention in Long Beach, California, because the Ventura faction wanted the convention held in Minnesota. Meanwhile, Donald Trump had arranged to meet with Ventura to discuss a possible Trump run for the Reform Party presidential nomination. At the same time, Pat Buchanan was campaigning for the support of Perot backers in his run for the presidential Reform Party nomination. It was clear: as the Reform Party grew in importance—and qualified for $12.6 million in federal funding—divisions within the party exploded, and outsiders suddenly appeared to court the party members.

Formation of the Reform Leadership Council (RfLC)

Most of the party officials elected in 1997, who would soon be leaving office, were discussing these divisions within the Reform Party. To stay together as a cohesive "interest" group, we departing officials decided to form an independent organization that we called the Reform Leadership Council (RfLC). Gerry Moan was on this council. He had been elected as vice chairman of RPUSA under Jack Gargan. Russ Verney and the entire (still legally in office) 1997-elected Executive Committee were in this discussion as well.

All of us agreed that Jack Gargan, who had not yet taken office, was already overstepping his responsibilities and ignoring the party members, the National Committee, and the Executive Committee.

What had happened to Jack Gargan, the man who encouraged Ross Perot to run for president in 1990 before millions of other Americans recognized Perot's value? This "different" Jack appeared to come alive after being elected chairman of the Reform Party. It looked as if Jack Gargan had moved away from the man who, in 1990, had placed effective newspaper ads. In these ads, Jack declared that voters at every election should remove all incumbents, until elected officials listened to the people.

In late January 2000, this apparent change in Jack led to the preparation of a draft paper entitled "Reasons to Consider the Removal of Jack Gargan as RPUSA Chairman." This draft was then circulated among RfLC members.

Also that January, Lenora Fulani publicly declared her support for Pat Buchanan—again seeming to follow her perception of where the money and votes were moving. This endorsement led to a Fulani supporter taking over as treasurer of the Reform Party at the 2000 Nashville meeting.

2000 Nashville RPUSA National Committee meeting

On February 12, 2000, the RPUSA National Committee of the Reform Party held a special meeting in Nashville, Tennessee, to consider charges of misconduct against Jack Gargan. These charges were detailed in a paper entitled "Reasons to Consider the Removal of Jack Gargan as RPUSA Chairman." Some of these charges are listed below in this excerpt from the paper:

> ... Jack Gargan removed Mr. Farris from his position as Chair of the Presidential Nominations Committee stating that Gargan had the unbridled right to appoint and remove Committee chairs.
>
> While the National Chair does have the authority to appoint Committee chairs, Gargan failed to recognize that a higher authority, the National Convention, elected Mr. Farris to his position and therefore only the National Convention could remove him. According to the Constitution (Article V, Section 1 (b)) the National Chairman is bound to carry out the "actions of the National Convention."
>
> In addition, Mr. Gargan has acted to appoint John Talbot as Chair of the Presidential Nominations Committee. This would be a violation of the Rules for nomination of the Presidential and Vice-Presidential Candidates approved by two National Conventions.
>
> Under these Rules Section 11(2), it states that "... Changes in the membership and size of the Presidential Nominations Committee shall by unanimous vote of the Nominations Committee." This provision was an approved amendment at the Dearborn convention [in 1999] to specifically assure the integrity of the Committee charged with overseeing the nominations process.
>
> ... Presidential Nominations Process: By an overwhelming majority the democratically elected delegates to both the 1999 Dearborn Convention and to the 1998 Convention in Atlanta approved the procedures outlined by the Presidential Nominations Committee for the nomination of our party's presidential nominee. As our rules require, our National Officers are to abide by the decisions of the convention delegates. Mr. Gargan's repeated refusal to support, and his stated opposition to this process, is in violation of the binding and democratic vote of the delegates of two conventions.
>
> Mr. Gargan has repeatedly made statements saying that he does not support the process because it cannot work and that it must be changed. Although he has not said how it must be changed, he has made statements purposely designed to undermine the process (e.g. Boston Globe, 9/14/99: Gargan said, "We will have no way of knowing whether they [the voters] are in an insane asylum or in prison or 13 years old.") He has made public statements to the media and at the American Reform Party (a different alternative political party) convention where he described the nominations process as

being "crazy" and "this is life and death for the party." In sum, Gargan has made clear that he does not support the democratic decisions of the delegates to two RPUSA National Conventions, although as National Chairman he is legally bound to do so.

... Executive Committee Decisions: The Executive Committee is authorized under our Constitution to make binding decisions for the Reform Party. One such binding decision was to hold the 2000 National Convention in California. Whether one agrees or disagrees with the decision is immaterial to the legal obligation of our National Officers to abide by the decisions of the Executive Committee. Instead of abiding by their decision, Jack Gargan has made outrageous public statements calling the legally binding vote "illegal" (although he has yet to provide any evidence of purported illegality).

Mr. Gargan has chosen to support a claim by two state chairmen to move the 2000 National convention to Minnesota. He has therefore supported an illegal mail-in vote that failed to obtain a verifiable quorum at that never held meeting. In addition, Gargan proclaimed during an Executive Committee teleconference on January 9, 2000 that he had in his possession information which "conclusively, irrevocably, and by any measurement indicated" that the mail-in vote was valid. He committed to supplying the Executive Committee with this proof immediately. To date, this proof has not been supplied despite numerous requests. Gargan's express opposition to the constitutionally binding Executive Committee vote is an additional violation of his legally binding obligations as a National Officer.

... Executive Committee Meetings: According to our party constitution, any three members of the Executive Committee may call an emergency Executive Committee meeting. (See Article V, Section 8: "Executive Committee meetings may be called ... upon action of any three Executive Committee members.") Such a meeting was properly called and notified for January 9, 2000. Upon receiving the notification, Gargan responded, "As for me, I refuse to preside over (or attend) this outrageous mockery of democratic principles."

Another emergency Executive Committee meeting was properly called and notified for January 18, 2000, again according to Party rules. Gargan called in but refused to call the meeting to order and left the call.

The following day, Gargan wrote in an e-mail, "This entire 'meeting' was null and void according to our constitution and RROO [Robert's Rules of Order]." He claimed that if he, as Chairman, did not call the meeting to order, then there was no official meeting. In addition, Mr. Gargan was interviewed in the American Reporter the following day saying, "I've ruled that there will be regular and open meetings and that emergency meetings were illegal." This action clearly defies the RPUSA Constitution that any three members can call an emergency meeting.

According to Tom McLaughlin, State Chairman of Pennsylvania and former National Rules Committee chairman: "Both Phil Madsen (current National Rules Committee Chairman) and I were actually on the conference call in question. The meeting was properly called by the three Executive Committee members, per RPUSA Constitution Article V, Section 8. With the meeting properly called, the full Executive Committee was present through their own actions—they had to call in from their telephones. The Chairman left. A quorum was still present. In the absence of the Chairman, the Vice Chairman called the meeting to order. (Note: discussions had taken place and a vote was taken during the conference call and that discussion was presided over by the National chairman before the National Chairman decided to declare the meeting invalid based upon a non-applicable notice requirement.) Mr. Madsen was present throughout the meeting except for short periods of time when he was talking on his other telephone line. Phil stated more than once that he was trying to get Jack to come back to the conference call."

... Interference in State Party Business: Mr. Gargan has interfered and undermined democratically elected leaders in state organizations. He has supported and encouraged Reform Party members in various states to go against the democratically elected leadership in spite of his duty as an Executive Committee member to "carry on the successful operation of the Reform Party" (See Article V, Section 1).

The remaining portions of the case presented against Jack Gargan at the February 12, 2000 meeting include: misconduct, failure to uphold the duties of his office, failure to demonstrate loyalty to the Reform Party, failure to act in a dignified and responsible manner, failure to keep his promises to the Reform Party members, and failure to uphold the highest moral and ethical standards.

The document's conclusion states:

Mr. Gargan has not only violated our Constitution but also our Principles. He has rendered himself unwilling to follow the democratic mandates of the Party. He has failed to uphold the duties and responsibilities of the office of National Chairman. By so doing Jack Gargan has unequivocally failed the very people who elected him to this office.

Given that our Party stands for setting the highest ethical standards for our elected officials, we as a Party cannot stand idly by and allow this behavior to continue.

The most important act that we can commit this year as a Party is to unify behind our presidential candidate. We need a leader to unify the Party. We need a leader who will lead by example. We need a leader that we can trust. We need a leader who will reflect the standards of our party.

Given the evidence of this document, Jack Gargan is unfit to serve as National Chairman of the Reform Party of the United States of America.

A vote of the members of the National Committee of the RPUSA was taken after they reviewed this paper. The final numbers were 109 to 31 in favor of removing Jack Gargan as the chairman of the National Reform Party.

I wasn't able to personally attend this meeting because of my husband's medical condition. He was in the middle of treatments to destroy a brain tumor and I didn't want to leave him. Thankfully, his treatment was successful, and in my opinion so was the meeting.

Media coverage

The press heavily covered the Nashville meeting. In addition, there were many comments by RPUSA members who attended.

For example, one Associated Press article ran under the headline "Reform Party ousts chairman in raucous meeting." The article pointed out that Jack Gargan was "an ally of dissident Jesse Ventura." The reporter continued, "During a showdown yesterday [the meeting attendees] exploded with raw hostility and scuffling.... Dale Welch Barlow, a Gargan ally [and former interim vice chair who was voted out of office in November 1997] jumped on stage in front of Gargan and hollered at his detractors; 'I am ashamed of this party.' ... At one point, a Perot ally who identified herself as Melanie of San Diego rushed the front of the room and tried to unplug Gargan's microphone because he wouldn't call the meeting to order."

The report continues, "Sue Harris de Bauche of Virginia [wife of the RPUSA Treasurer Ron Young, who was later removed from office] slapped and pushed Melanie to the floor, and two police officers separated them. One escorted Harris de Bauche from the room, as it rang with members telling each other to 'shut up' and begin the meeting." Donna Donovan, spokeswoman for the Perot faction, said, "Democracy can be messy, can't it?"

Gargan removed

The Associated Press article pointed out that "The [RPUSA National] Committee, by a 109–31 vote, ousted Gargan on a motion that said 'he has failed to faithfully perform and execute the duties of his office.' The motion said Gargan's failures and violations of the party's constitution 'have resulted in substantial harm to the public image of the party, and in a breakdown of the proper administration, operation and governance of the party.'" The charges against Gargan were laid out for committee members, the press, and the public in the "Reasons for Removal" hand out presented earlier.

On Friday, February 12, 2000, Jesse Ventura, the governor of Minnesota, quit the Reform Party. Jesse stated, "This was not the Reform Party I knew. This is not the party of honesty and integrity."

These words were from a man whose comments in the November 1999 issue of *Playboy* focused on "overweight people, drugs, prostitution, women's undergarments and many other subjects," as stated in Russ Verney's letter to Ventura, which is displayed in full in chapter 12. That letter, sent to Jesse Ventura from the RPUSA Executive Committee on October 1, 1999, also stated, "You have brought shame to yourself and disgrace to the members of the Reform Party." The letter also suggested that Jesse resign from the Reform Party "for the good of the members."

The members got their way on February 12 when Ventura announced his resignation from the party, and again on February 13, when Jack Gargan and Ron Young were removed from office.

The National Committee members reaffirmed the location for the RPUSA 2000 Presidential Nominating Convention as Long Beach, California, and picked Pat Choate to be the new RPUSA chairman, with Gerry Moan remaining as vice chairman. However, Pat Choate only held office for a few weeks before having to resign. His wife's son had developed cancer, and Pat needed to devote himself to his wife and help care for his stepson. At that point, Gerry Moan became the acting chairman of RPUSA.

Members respond with different perspectives

When Diane McKelvey, a National Committee delegate from Michigan, was asked what she thought of the Nashville meeting, she replied, "What did I think of the meeting ...? Let's see ... members of a state delegation who had been with the movement since 1992 were not seated. The National Chairman refused to call the meeting to order; chanting and yelling went on; Dale Barlow went bonkers; sound was disconnected; Melanie was almost in a fight; the Assistant Secretary stormed off of the stage and verbally assaulted a member of her own state party; the police were called; Gargan was removed as National Chairman. It was fantastic!"

Another member, Jeff McCloskey from Pennsylvania, saw this meeting from a different perspective. He stated, "It always amazes me how repeated telling of a story can cause it to be blown well out of proportion in relation to the actual event. This is no exception."

Jeff continued, "The National Committee meeting in Nashville had been called for the explicit purpose of removing Jack Gargan from his position as national chairman of RPUSA. As anyone who has ever belonged to any type of civic organization can tell you, the duty of the chairman is to follow the will of the membership. In our case, Mr. Gargan convinced himself he could totally ignore any instructions given to him by anyone in the party—including the national convention, which elected him in the first place. Sensing the problems that would be brought about by a rogue chairman doing his own thing, the Nashville meeting was called in order to remove him and put someone in the position who understood the job's requirements."

Jeff pointed out, "If the Republicans or Democrats realized they made a mistake in party leadership and made a change, that would be considered a normal justified step. But, since we're the Reform Party, it's news."

Then, referring to the adjective "raucous," Jeff said, "Oh, as to the 'brawl,' I suspect within a year or so I'll be reading about the major riot that took place in Nashville."

Jeff presented a much less sensationalist view of the proceedings. He stated, "At the beginning of the Nashville meeting, Jack Gargan stood up at the mic and went into a long rambling explanation of why he wouldn't allow the meeting to happen. Jack is well known for monopolizing the floor, allowing nobody else to get a word in edgewise. The decision was made to unplug Mr. Gargan's microphone, hoping that would help to calm everyone down. One woman went up to unplug the microphone, and another, taking offense at the action, pushed her down and slapped her shoulders as she fell. That, in total, was the great brawl I've heard so much about. The police then quickly scooted both women out—neither wanted to press charges—and the woman who had pushed the other down voluntarily agreed not to return to the meeting hall."

Jeff summed it up, saying, "That's the real, untold story. A minor altercation followed by one person agreeing not to return. No brawl, no wrestling match, no delegate ejections, just lots of editorial writers drooling over the chance to make much ado about nothing. What has never been reported is the seven to eight hours of peaceful, deliberate discussions that took place after the meeting had finally come to order. But then, that wouldn't be anywhere near as interesting to read as the 'brawl' that never was."

Thus had begun the changing of the RPUSA guard—from Ventura supporters Jack Gargan and Ron Young, to Buchanan supporters Pat Choate and Gerry Moan.

But there were more changes in store. The ultimate split took place at the 2000 RPUSA Presidential Nominating Convention in Long Beach, California.

Chapter 14

2000: Changing of the Guard, Continued

Preparing for the RPUSA Presidential Nominating Convention

The six months between the removal of Jack Gargan in February and the August 2000 RPUSA Presidential Nominating Convention were occupied by Gargan trying to deny the legality of his removal, Pat Buchanan campaigning for the RPUSA presidential nomination, and organizing the Long Beach convention.

Gargan lost his battle. Pat Buchanan won his. And the Reform Party was nearing its last gasp as a major political force.

Buchanan supporters move into state parties

Then at the convention, in order to be seated, a vote of the delegates would be needed to determine which group was recognized as the legitimate state affiliate of the national Reform Party. Clearly, the idea was to stack the nominating convention with Buchanan delegates (chosen by nationally recognized affiliated state parties) who would then support and vote for Buchanan as the Reform Party presidential nominee.

According to Russ Verney, the former chairman of RPUSA, "A report published by the Chicago-based Center for New Community which tracks hate groups, many white separatist and anti-Semitic organizations including the Aryan Nation, the Storm Troopers, the American Friends of the British Nationalist Party, the Council of Conservative Citizens, and others, were using the Internet and other means of communication to urge their followers to join the Reform Party to support Pat Buchanan's candidacy. At least three candidates for public office through state Reform Parties [taken over by the Buchanan Brigades] openly campaigned as white supremacists and general bigots."

Russ continued, "The incidence of intimidation at Reform Party meetings, in anonymous telephone calls and via the Internet reached frightening levels, including death threats."

In addition, attempts were being made to "redo" the Executive Committee by removing people who did not support Buchanan, like Lou Ann Jones of Montana and Paul Truax of Texas.

In order to try to control the legitimate Credentials Committee, the Buchanan cadre offered Dot Drew of North Carolina, the leader of that committee, a paid position. She declined.

At the same time, using the votes she controlled, Lenora Fulani from New York City wrote to Buchanan asking, as one of her demands, that she be tapped to replace Gerry Moan as the Reform Party chair. Pat Buchanan sent her an e-mail explaining why that could not happen. That decision by Buchanan was one more act leading to the eventual convention chaos in Long Beach.

All of these deals and maneuvers put a lot of pressure on Dot Drew and her convention credentialing committee, and eventually led to a lockdown of the entire committee.

Credentialing becomes an issue

Creating a fair and thorough credentialing process had always been crucial to the running of a successful convention. This process had to be more detailed and thorough than ever before due to the increase in factions, and widening split between the groups. In addition, continuing updates were important as the Buchanan supporters were moving into leadership positions within the state parties. In fact, as of July 12, 2000, we were still adding members to the Credentials Committee in an attempt to have all groups represented. We ended with fifteen members and representatives from all factions. However, like any group, only a few people did most of the preparation and were actually at the credentials table when the convention began.

I worked closely with Dot Drew on developing a fair, representative procedure. It took hours, days, and months of our time, along with the help of state leadership across the country. During each RPUSA convention, there were challenges within the states. But even before the 2000 convention convened, the entire Credentials Committee itself was challenged.

The "sham" party primary

At the same time that the credentialing process was being organized, a Reform Party Primary was being held. Only two candidates qualified—Pat Buchanan and John Hagelin (who was also the presidential candidate of the Natural Law Party).

The primary process became an issue when arguments developed over the legitimacy of the Buchanan primary votes. The Executive Committee met and called for an audit of the primary ballots. Hagelin ballots were declared legal, but Buchanan refused an audit. Therefore, the Buchanan ballots could not be verified.

At this point, Gerry Moan, the RPUSA acting chairman, declared the Executive Committee meeting (that called for an audit) invalid because he, along with two other people, had not been in attendance. Therefore, Gerry claimed the quorum requirement had not been met. Yet another argument ensued over whether the chairman counted as part of the quorum.

Gerry's next step on July 12, 2000, was to send an e-mail removing Beverly Kennedy as the "Chairman's parliementarian" [sic], which was Gerry's bestowed title for Bev's position.

This disagreement, and the goal to seat Buchanan supporters as convention delegates, led to Gerry Moan's call for an emergency National Committee meeting on August 8, 2000, in Long Beach—two days before the RPUSA Presidential Nominating Convention.

National Committee meeting in Long Beach

I was not a member of the National Committee, and therefore was not invited to participate in the meeting. However, the following section depicts the events as presented to me by those who did attend, including Gerry Moan and Jim Mangia.

According to those who were there, Gerry Moan called the National Committee meeting to order. Gerry had moved into the RPUSA acting chairman position when Pat Choate, who was the elected chairman, had to resign in April 2000 because of a family illness. The meeting agenda focused on the seating of members of the Buchanan Freedom Party, a political party structure set up in states where the Buchanan supporters could not take over the RPUSA-affiliated state parties. It was clear that this meeting was called to make sure the Buchanan supporters were seated as "legal" delegates, replacing state delegates from the legitimate RPUSA-affiliated state parties. In fact, the names from the Freedom Party groups had been illegally submitted to the Credentials Committee before the convention. The legal Credentials Committee members were identifying these illegal names as unqualified to attend or vote because they did not belong to the RPUSA-affiliated state parties.

Since the majority of elected National Committee members who appeared at the convention were from the official RPUSA affiliated state parties, Gerry Moan had a problem. To "solve" this problem, Gerry simply declared that the Freedom Party Buchanan supporters would be the delegates seated at the RPUSA Presidential Nominating Convention.

In fact, the independent professional parliamentarian (who was hired by Gerry Moan and the Buchanan leadership to replace Beverly Kennedy) told Moan his move was illegal. Moan simply told the parliamentarian that she only advised him, and he made the decisions. Gerry overruled the parliamentarian's ruling and she angrily walked out.

When I recently asked Gerry about this action, his statement was, simply, "I did what needed to be done."

Since Gerry refused to follow the parliamentarian's ruling, a large group led by Jim Mangia from California also walked out, leaving the meeting without a quorum to continue. But, according to Gerry, the meeting was legitimate because the delegates he had (illegally) personally approved voted without a quorum to create a quorum!

Are you still with me?

The RPUSA-elected secretary, Jim Mangia, presented the following view of what he saw and heard at that National Committee meeting:

"The credentialing and verifying process for the National Committee had been handled traditionally by the National Secretary (as it had been done at all previous National Committee meetings, including the meeting in Nashville a few months earlier when Gargan was removed). However, in Long Beach, Gerry Moan refused to allow me [the national secretary] access to the National Committee list. He opened the meeting and proceeded to refuse to announce which states were credentialed and which delegates were representing various states. It was like a circus, a free-for-all. Anytime anyone would say anything opposing something Moan and the Buchanan [supporters] ... wanted to do, they would shout us down. It was chaos."

Jim continued, "I remember that there were many people in the room who were not Reform Party members and did not have the right to vote. Moan would call for a voice vote—and they would never count the votes. One such vote credentialed everyone in the room (by voice), but he refused to provide the list. The parliamentarian who we had hired to preside over the process made several rulings which Moan refused to recognize, and she left in disgust."

Mangia said, "Buchanan's security team would not allow credentialed National Committee delegates into the room who opposed Buchanan, including Russ Verney. It was clear that there would be no democratic process. I announced that this was a sham, the meeting was illegal, the delegates had not been credentialed properly and the Chair (Gerry Moan) would not abide by the rulings of the parliamentarian, and that we should walk out."

Jim explains, "We exited to a phalanx of television cameras and reporters, and I began a spontaneous demonstration outside of the hall about the theft of the [Reform] Party and how they'd trampled every Reform Party rule and every basic tenet of Robert's Rules. It was a farce. We marched to the main hall and held a demonstration. Hundreds of delegates joined to protest the ... illegal and undemocratic tactics of Moan and the Buchanan delegates."

He said, "The next day, we all marched together to the convention hall to be seated (singing 'We Shall Overcome') and we were locked out. They would not let us enter the convention hall—hundreds of delegates. This was covered in the NY Times with a centerfold photo spread showing us being locked out and refused entry into the convention hall."

Credentialing Committee lockdown

After cooking up a credentialing stew at the RPUSA National Committee meeting, Gerry Moan then chose to meddle with the Credentials Committee that was organized for the convention itself.

Before the convention was to begin, Dot Drew was unilaterally "removed" by Gerry Moan as credentials chairman and replaced by Frank Reed of Ohio, a Buchanan supporter. Dot refused to accept Gerry's dismissal of her. Those on Dot's committee who supported Buchanan had moved over to Frank Reed's group. Reform Party members supporting John Hagelin, or simply against Buchanan, remained with Dot, including me.

At 5:30 a.m. on the morning the credentialing of delegates was about to begin, Dot Drew, anticipating trouble (boy, was she right!), went over to the convention center and began setting up the credentials room. Her committee members began arriving and preparing to certify delegates to the convention. Soon Dale Cooter, the lawyer working with the Buchanan campaign, appeared along with other Buchanan supporters, and they attempted to remove us from the credentialing room. Dot refused to budge. Convention security was placed outside the door to the room to keep delegates from credentialing with this committee. Meanwhile, the "other," Frank Reed—led, Buchanan Credentialing Committee was set up in a different room, closer to the convention auditorium.

In between the two rooms was a group hired to provide administrative services to the Credentials Committee. They, like many RPUSA delegates, were caught in the middle of a major schism within the party.

Hours later, Gerry Moan came to our room to talk with Dot. Gerry is a rather imposing man, and he walked up to Dot and leaned in quite close to her face. She immediately reacted and said she felt threatened by him. Regardless of how she felt, Dot refused to leave, and said so loud and clear. The rest of us stood behind her and held our ground.

Outside of this room the press had gotten wind of the "locked down" event. They began to mass outside of the closed door leading to Dot's group. Security prevented them and anyone else from entering. One interesting fact is that the individual who had been selected to be head of convention security, Alec McKelvey, a retired Michigan state trooper, was (and still is) the husband of Diane McKelvey, one of the people locked in the room. Alec was one of the two men guarding the door.

Eventually, a convention center employee unlocked the back entrance to the room. At that point, Diane asked Alec to open the door and let the press in since we now had a way out if we chose to take it, and we began to speak with the media.

After the interviews, Dot and our group met and decided to set up a table outside of the room we had vacated, where we continued credentialing delegates out in the open. Many state delegates came to our table and signed in through our Credentials Committee. We had the original list and all of the material needed by the delegates for proper credentialing.

I saw some delegates heading for Frank Reed's "credentialing room." In fact, I began to see many delegates registering with both credentialing groups. Clearly, no one was sure what was happening. The attendees were covering all bases to make sure they were registered as delegates for the convention.

Buchanan-run New Jersey Reform Party members had elected me as a delegate to the 2000 RPUSA Presidential Nominating Convention. Therefore, I should have been allowed to register with the Frank Reed credentialing group. However, I was barred from that room and was given excuse after excuse for two hours as to why I couldn't register, such as, "the members are taking a break," or, "the line is too long to let anyone else in the room." Yet, according to Bev Kidder, a seat was being held for me in the Buchanan convention by the New Jersey delegation.

Meanwhile, an entire group of delegates led by Jim Mangia, some who were barred from the Buchanan convention and others who had decided that was not the place they wanted to be, marched out of the convention building down the street to another venue in the conference complex. That new location had been found and paid for by a group of people the evening after the now-infamous National Committee meeting. Another Reform Party convention was being held there, and the Reform Party candidate was going to be John Hagelin from the Natural Law Party.

Since Dot's Credentialing Committee had all of the duly elected names of delegates approved by each state, we were invited to move with the group over to the new location and credential the delegates for the Hagelin convention. And we went.

The Hagelin convention

We began and completed the credentialing process. At the same time this activity was taking place, we later learned there was a "smoke-filled room" meeting going on. Attending the meeting were representatives from the Perot support group, the Fulani activists, and the Hagelin representatives. The people at this meeting agreed upon a slate of candidates to lead the Reform Party and run the convention. Once the decision was made, they lobbied the delegates to support this slate, and these individuals were elected. The treasurer was Harry Kresky from the Fulani group. According to a meeting attendee, Mr. Kresky was chosen because he was a lawyer who agreed to handle national court cases for Hagelin gratis. Dror Bar-Sadeh from the Perot group was chosen as the nominee for Reform Party secretary. And, most surprising of all, the Hagelin group supported Sue de Bauche Young for vice chairman—the woman married to the former Reform Party Treasurer Ron Young, who had been removed from office in early 2000 along with Jack Gargan. Jim Mangia, a Fulani supporter, was elected convention and party chairman.

Jim Mangia's first step when the convention opened was to seat the delegates. At that point I realized the "fix" was in for a slate agreed upon as a compromise among the leaders of the various groups, without input from the membership. This convention had begun to smell like a Democratic or Republican convention—maybe worse.

What had happened? We had given up—lost our way. We had become part of the broken system instead of persisting in trying to fix it.

The final straw came for me when the "chosen" New Jersey chairman refused to recognize me as a delegate. At that point I turned to my husband and said, "Let's go sightseeing."

I left the convention with a heavy heart and in somewhat of a daze. What had happened to the movement I had joined in 1992 with such hope for our country's future? What had happened to ethics and commitment to fairness and grassroots participation?

Two conventions continue

Meanwhile, both conventions continued. In fact, one delegate, an attorney and the chairman of the Massachusetts Reform Party, Andy Lizotte, was able to attend both. He arrived Friday evening not realizing there were "dueling" conventions. Andy went into the Buchanan convention hall and said, "In ten minutes I recognized it was a Buchanan love fest." He stayed for two hours and noticed that, "People hostile to Buchanan had left the building." He watched as Fulani supporters marched into the hall, gave an anti-Buchanan speech, and walked out en masse. At that point, he realized there was another convention down the street. Several Massachusetts delegates stayed at the Buchanan convention, while others left. Although Andy agreed with Buchanan on several issues, he left that venue and went to see and hear what was taking place at the Hagelin convention.

In fact, at the urging of some delegates, he wound up running for Reform Party treasurer against Harry Kresky. Of course, neither he, nor those who encouraged him to run, knew the decision had already been made behind closed doors that Kresky was going to be the new Reform Party treasurer.

Buchanan versus Hagelin in the 2000 election

After the 2000 Reform Party conventions, the chaos moved to the courts, as discussed in the following chapter. The election itself was barely a blip as far as Buchanan's and Hagelin's impact was concerned.

John Hagelin had very little media coverage and was forced to run representing the Natural Law Party, rather than the Reform Party. Pat Buchanan had use of the $12.6 million in federal funds that Perot and the Reform Party had qualified for from the 1996 presidential election. However, Pat Buchanan only spent money in states that were not heavily contested between Bush and Gore, and his media advertising was scant at best. Also, he became ill during the campaign and had to have surgery, limiting his campaigning time.

The election showing of both Hagelin and Buchanan was abysmal. Voting tallies for each of these candidates came in at less than one half of 1 percent.

Is the "Party" over?

No. Although greatly diminished in size and influence, the Reform Party continues to exist and function in some states. Several Reform Party local and state organizations have run candidates for office. For example, former Colorado state chairman Victor Good ran for Congress in 2000 and 2002 and for the senate in 2004. In 2006, Eric Eidsness, of Colorado, ran for Congress. Max Linn ran for governor of Florida in 2006. In 2007, Janice Miller was the vice mayor of Oldsmar, Florida, holding office for four years with two more years to go. She will then be term-limited out of office. In 2006, Diane McKelvey ran as a Republican for township clerk of Colon, Michigan, (handling elections as well as other duties), and won.

Also, the Reform Party is growing as people from other political parties change registration. As disgust grows with the extremist control in both major political parties, new Reform Party members are coming from the Republicans and Democrats. A political party change occurred in Florida when Tom Macklin, a Republican, resigned as mayor of Avon Park Florida to run with Max Linn as the Reform Party candidate for lieutenant governor. He brought with him several other new Reform Party members.

In addition, people who became energized by the 1992 expansion of the reform movement have continued to participate in the political process. For example, Nikki Love (remember the fourteen-year-old from Hawaii?), who volunteered in the 1992 Perot for President campaign, is continuing her involvement in local politics. She now sits on a committee that is restructuring her town government.

It also needs to be noted that people who were politically awakened in 1992 and 1996 by Ross Perot's presidential runs for office have joined the Democrats and Republicans as well. They became, and remain, active participants in the political process.

Those of us who participated in the Perot reform movement from 1992 through today have learned from our mistakes. There are people still involved in Reform Party state organizations. They continue to develop growth strategies and work to expand the party. At this point, they are mainly building at the local level, as well as the county and state levels. Time, hard work, tenacity, and the American people will determine the future success of the Reform Party and how American citizens will become involved in the running of our government.

Chapter 15

The People's Court?

Politics in the courts

One method of trying to impact the political process is through the courts. Court cases continue to be pursued in order to clarify election rules and requirements at all levels of government. For example, it is each state's election officials who determine ballot access requirements. As related earlier, the courts were kept busy after various state officials tried to prevent Ross Perot's name from appearing on their state election ballots in 1996. Several alternative political parties, including the Reform Party, are still using the courts to try to force state legislatures to equalize the ballot access requirements for all political candidates, including people running as independents. However, sometimes, individual political candidates use the courts to thwart the system.

The 2000 election

For example, after the Long Beach convention and the split in the Reform Party, Pat Buchanan used the courts to try to get his name on state ballots as the RPUSA presidential candidate in states where duly elected delegates had been locked out of the "Buchanan" convention.

Michigan was one state where a lawsuit was filed. Diane McKelvey experienced the use of the courts by Pat Buchanan, as she was peppered with threats and intimidation. She stated, "Things in Michigan really started to heat up as soon as I got back from the Long Beach convention."

Diane continued, "Eleanor Renfrew, the Michigan Reform Party Secretary, and I turned in John Hagelin's name as the Reform Party candidate for President. At the same time, a rump Buchanan bunch turned in the name of Pat Buchanan. This left the Michigan Secretary of State with a dilemma—which name goes on the ballot? The Secretary of State's office contacted me and asked for complete documentation of our meetings, conventions, state committee members, and a host of other items—which they wanted by 4:00 p.m. the next day."

Diane still doesn't know how she did it, and she explained that, "I stayed up for over 24 hours getting all of the documentation together, including the illegal meetings, dates, and bogus delegates that the Buchanan bunch had put together and faxed it to them as requested by 4:00 p.m. the next day. I was exhausted, both physically and mentally. That, however, was not the end of it. I was sent another laundry list of documentation wanted by the Michigan Secretary of State, again due by 4:00 p.m. the following day. This, too, got done and I breathed a sigh of relief when I didn't hear from them again."

She then goes on, "The relief was short lived however. In a few days I received a long letter which essentially said it wasn't the job of the Secretary of State to determine who the candidate was and that it was an intra-party problem for us to solve."

After this, Diane stated, "[I] was at a loss to know what to do. These Buchanan supporters were unrelenting people. They professed to be Christians, but their actions belied the honesty and morality of true Christians. I found out that they would go to extreme lengths to get what they wanted. In fact, I received a phone call from a man who wanted to talk to me about the Buchanan nomination. I agreed to meet with him, but at a public place where I could also bring my husband. He was a quiet-spoken man who said he had worked for Buchanan in the past. We talked for about an hour during which he continually tried to convince me to withdraw Hagelin's name and join the Buchanan campaign. I said I would give some consideration to what he had to say. But when he called me the next day I told him that I could not in good conscience do what he was asking of me. I told him that Ross Perot had always said to adhere to the highest ethical standards, and that agreeing to what he wanted would compromise those standards. I actually thought that was the end of it. Not to be. He started calling me on a daily basis."

Diane then received the real surprise. She explained, "On the Friday before Labor Day in the late afternoon, a process server showed up at my door. The Buchanan bunch was suing the Secretary of State and me, with a court date set for the next week. This gave me no opportunity to find a lawyer until the following Tuesday, since all offices were closed on Monday. Quite clever on their part. In fact, I didn't know who or where to get an attorney."

Diane called Russ Verney, former chairman of RPUSA, in Dallas. Russ suggested that Diane get in touch with Hagelin's attorney, since Hagelin had a stake in this. Diane put the call through but could only leave a message. She said, "I think Russ also called him, because when the attorney called me back he already had some knowledge of the situation. Later that afternoon, Hagelin's attorney called again and said he had an attorney for me and I would soon get a call from him. A few minutes later the phone rang and it was the attorney whose name was George Washington. Was this a good omen or what? Due to his schedule George could not meet with me until the next evening—Wednesday night. The court date was Friday morning."

Diane and her husband Alec met with George Washington on Wednesday evening, with all of her documentation. According to Diane, "Mr. Washington said that we did not have a very good chance of getting Hagelin on the ballot under the Reform Party banner (Hagelin already had access to the ballot through the Natural Law Party) but he believed we could block Buchanan. I told him we had to try."

Diane felt a sense of relief, believing it was now out of her hands. But Buchanan's people were not about to stop. The following day, Diane said, "I got the first of a long line of threatening phone calls. Mostly they were brief like, 'back off' or 'I know where you live' and they would immediately hang up. These occurrences made me a nervous wreck by Friday. George Washington and I went to court together. I kept my hands under the table because they were shaking so hard. I prayed that George would not call me to the stand. I don't think I could have walked that far. As the case began, I relaxed somewhat. In my opinion, the presentation of the opposing attorney was not very good. But then, perhaps it was because he didn't have a lot to work with."

Diane continued, "As it turned out, I didn't have to testify. The judge heard all sides of the argument and then called a recess to make his decision. Finally, the judge came back and we were asked to stand as he read his decision. As I stood, I had to lean on the table because my knees were shaking so hard I didn't think they would support me. My heart was pounding so hard that I was surprised that the entire courtroom didn't hear it. At last the judge got to the meat of the decision. He stated that the bulk of the evidence favored McKelvey, and the judge denied Buchanan ballot access on the Reform Party ticket. He also denied Hagelin but that didn't matter since I was expecting that to happen. I had to stop myself from doing a cartwheel right then and there! I beat Buchanan, and did the right thing."

However, Diane's elation was short lived. She said, "A few days later the process server showed up with another subpoena. The Buchanan bunch was taking it to appeals court. We again prevailed in that court but the decision was 2–1 in my favor. This shook my confidence some but I was still on the winning side."

And still her story did not end. Diane continued, "We went through about nine courts until the deadline came to get the name printed on the ballot. I got to know the process server on a first name basis, learned about his wife and kids, and each time he showed up he apologized. The last court it went to was the U.S. Supreme Court where they threw it out."

While this court fight was going on, Diane was getting threatening phone calls, e-mails from white supremacists, and she even had a stalker. In fact, she said, "Alec wouldn't allow me to go anywhere by myself. Wherever I went, he went. On top of it all, the 'Buchanan man' again showed up on my doorstep. I was absolutely furious. I had several words for him, none of which can be repeated in polite company. He left forthwith after I threatened to turn my dog on him. My dog was extremely vicious and snarling at him through the glass door."

At last, Diane continued, "the deadline passed and Buchanan did not get a ballot line in Michigan. The state allowed him on as a write-in candidate. He received 1800 votes. I'm sure the dog catcher received more."

Diane had two observations regarding this experience. She stated, "One— George Washington did a stupendous job. He had very little preparation time and ran rings around the opposition. He was a class act with an outstanding courtroom demeanor. Two— politicians using our court system and other tactics are not going to allow any competition in the elections unless people stand up and push for change. The deck was stacked against us from the beginning. Another learning experience."

A second example of how the courts were used took place in Connecticut. Donna Donovan, the Reform Party of Connecticut state chairman, had an experience similar to Diane's in Michigan. There were two groups calling themselves the Reform Party. The Donovan team submitted the names of Hagelin/Goldhaber to the secretary of state as the Reform Party presidential and vice presidential ticket. The other group submitted Buchanan/Foster for the same spot. This situation also went to court when Buchanan people once again brought suit to get Buchanan's name on the Reform Party ballot line. However, the result was different.

In Connecticut, the judge found that the Buchanan supporters, led by Floyd Atchley of West Haven, were not the real Reform Party, but rather the Reform Party was the group led by Donna Donovan. However, he ordered that Donovan's group submit, and the secretary of state place Buchanan's name under the Reform Party on the election ballot. This reminds me of the story in the Bible where a man and a woman appear before King Solomon as judge, each demanding sole custody of the baby. King Solomon decided to compromise and cut the baby in half.

We'll never know why the Connecticut judge divided the "baby" in half. However, we do know the courts have been politicized, and judges are part of the political system. They are either elected, which makes them candidates running for office, or are appointed by politicians. Donna said that "Judge Francis M. McDonald, who presided over our case, was appointed to the state Supreme Court by Governor John Rowland, a Republican, who later served time in prison for taking 'gifts' from state contractors. In addition, at that time, Judge McDonald's son was running as a Republican for a seat in the state legislature. I guess the decision shouldn't have shocked me, but I did learn hope from Ross Perot, and hope dies hard."

"Judges are politicians"

In fact, Russ Verney, the former chairman of the national Reform Party, stated it simply, "Judges are politicians." Russ clarified, "In order to become a Federal District Court judge the candidate must be an attorney. The president has to nominate him or her and, under the advice and consent clause of the U.S. Constitution, the Senate must confirm the nomination."

Russ continued, "How do you get the President to nominate you? Simple, befriend your U.S. Senators. In fact, the senior Senator from the same political party as the President must propose and lobby the President to enter your name into nomination for the judgeship."

Russ raised the next question, "How do you get a Senator to propose and lobby for you with the President and other Senators? By being actively involved in politics."

"We all would like to believe that our government does things because they are right and just actions," Russ continued. "Unfortunately, elected government officials do things with an eye to election and re-election and for the pursuit of their personal ambitions. Consequently, in order for a Senator to propose a name for a coveted judgeship with lifetime tenure, there has to be something in it for the Senator, like campaign support and contributions from the prospective judge and/or his/her advocate, plus a common political philosophy. Becoming a judge relies as much upon whom you know and your connections to elected politicians, as it does on your legal qualifications."

He added, "And politics doesn't end when you reach the level of Federal District Court Judge. The politicians in Congress govern the judicial profession. Congress determines all employment benefits, including pay. Therefore, a good working relationship between the judiciary and legislators is important. If you want to climb the career ladder to become an Appeals Court judge, once again one must be proposed by a Senator, nominated by the President, and confirmed by the Senate.

Russ explained, "Competition is more rigid for the Court of Appeals because generally the Court of Appeals covers more than one state, and, therefore, more then two Senators are competing to secure the nomination and confirmation of their protégés. Finally, the pinnacle of the profession is the U.S. Supreme Court, and especially Chief Justice. Again, the nominating process follows the same path discussed above. However, at this point, the political philosophy plays a bigger role in the political choice."

Continuing, Russ said, "A term that has entered everyday legal language is to be 'borked,' which refers to the Democratic Senate's rejection of a conservative judge, one-time Supreme Court nominee Robert Bork. More recently, President George W. Bush had to drop his pursuit of the nomination of White House Counsel Harriet Myers to the U.S. Supreme Court because she was not politically acceptable to a major portion of President Bush's core conservative supporters."

A clear example of the role the politicized judiciary plays in our political system was demonstrated during the 2000 presidential election. Russ commented, "Unfortunately, political considerations do not stop once someone is confirmed to the bench—even the U.S. Supreme Court bench. The decision in the Bush vs. Gore case in 2000 is a prime example. All five members of the Supreme court who traditionally support 'states' rights,' and the four members who support a more federal role, switched sides in this case."

Russ believes, "Elections, including the Presidential election are solely the business of the individual states, not the federal government. Yet, the 'states' rights' faction of the U.S. Supreme Court voted to overrule the Florida State Supreme Court, and the 'federalist' faction voted to uphold the Florida State Supreme Court. The outcome of that decision determined who could claim enough Electoral College votes nationwide to become the 43rd President. The Bush vs. Gore decision was such a philosophical reverse for all members of the U.S. Supreme Court that the decision starts out by stating that it cannot be used as precedent for any other future legal matter."

These are a few examples that demonstrate how politics plays a role in all three branches of government, including the judicial branch. To this day, issue organizations and political parties continue to file court cases to try to influence or change the election system or outcomes. There's no problem with using this tool. However, all parties must remember the courts and judges do not necessarily provide a fair and balanced decision, and are heavily influenced by party politics.

Chapter 16

The People's
Movement Continues

After the fiasco I experienced at the 2000 Reform Party convention in Long Beach, California, the growth of the Reform Party and the continued filing of court cases no longer interested me. Like a number of other Reform Party activists, I left Long Beach and mourned for a year.

Then, in June 2001, I stopped licking my wounds. More than twenty reform activists, including me, went to Maine to say good-bye to Lily Andrews, the former Maine Reform Party chairman, who was dying in the final stages of lung cancer. Lily had been very active in the reform movement from the beginning in 1992. She was an insistent voice of the people, a patriot, and a friend. She actually gave me my first birthday party at that gathering—a surprise party. We all had a wonderful time, including Lily. She died shortly after this get-together, on July 4, 2001—Independence Day. But her spirit still lives. She reminded me, and others, that the movement was not gone. In fact, the community still lived to flourish another day.

Thanks to Lily, I won't ever forget again, or stop hoping for a better future for our country. But I was still not ready to move forward.

In August 2001, I decided it was time to focus on my other life. In 1993 my husband and I moved to Cherry Hill, New Jersey. I quickly realized I had no time to think about, let alone decorate, our new home. I was too busy running my own recruiting business, caring for my husband during his battle with a brain tumor, continuing to support my two boys, and participating in the political reform movement begun in 1992 by Ross Perot. My living room and dining room didn't have any real furniture, only a metal table covered with political and issue-related material, two desks, and a computer.

Finally, in July 2001, I decided to finish furnishing and decorating my home and to convert an outside back porch into an office for my business. On September 11, 2001 at 8:45 a.m., I was standing in front of the television in my den with the contractor who was handling the construction. The telephone rang. It was my son Michael, who lived on Staten Island in New York City. He was screaming at me, "Turn on the television. Turn to CNN," which I did immediately. I saw one of the twin towers burning as he screamed, "We've been hit by terrorists." At that point his cell phone went dead.

9/11 inspires a new movement

Later I learned that when he called me that morning, Michael was on a bus traveling over the Verrazano Bridge from Staten Island to Brooklyn. He had a clear view of the airplane as it slammed into the first tower. Everyone on that bus knew this was not an accident, as they watched the plane fly directly into the structure.

Once the contractor and his crew saw the television picture of the plane slamming into the tower, they immediately left to get more information and see if any of their relatives had been impacted. I called my husband and other son Steven to let them know what had happened. We received a call from my husband's sister, Barbara. Her son, Jon, was working that day in those towers. For two hours we had no idea what happened to Jon, or to my friend, Roz Davis, who worked in a Wall Street building next to the towers.

Finally, that afternoon, we heard that Jon had been one of the last to get out of the tower, and Roz had left the area in time, and gotten back to her home on Staten Island.

On September 12, I finished shopping for furniture. However, I was becoming terribly depressed. I had lived in New York City from 1963 until 1986. I started with an apartment in Manhattan, moved to Brooklyn, and then to Staten Island. Both of my children had been born in Brooklyn. I couldn't believe what had been done to this majestic city.

In late September 2001, my two sons, my husband, and I went to see the ruins at Ground Zero. It was the holiest day of the year for Jewish people, Yom Kippur—the Day of Atonement. I felt it was where we needed to be at this particular time. When we arrived by subway, the pulverized concrete still hung in the air. You could still smell smoke and see a smoldering fire. At that point, I knew it had really happened, and wasn't just a scene on television. For me, that visit made what had happened really sink in.

From that moment on, I was angry. I knew I was going to either spend the rest of my life hiding in my bedroom, or do something to redirect my anger.

I began to spend days alone in my home, cultivating my anger. Then, in early October, I received a call from Donna Donovan. She told me she had spoken with Ross Perot, and he was furious about what had occurred on 9/11. Her words woke me up. I had to act, and do something to fix the problem.

Ross Perot had put together a one-page sheet for how the government, at all levels, should approach this disaster. I was able to get a copy of that list. These ideas got me thinking about how the American people, acting as volunteers, could also help to prepare the nation to deal with a real threat on American soil— terrorism.

Emergency preparedness in action

I took my first action at the local level. I approached the Erlton South Civic Association where I lived. I presented a plan to organize our neighborhood into an emergency communication hub. We would have representatives on every block, people who could be contacted when there was an emergency. These block leaders would go door-to-door to personally inform their neighbors. We would designate one person from the executive board as the contact with the police. This person would call four section leaders who would then contact the block leaders, and so on.

This was to be set up as a two-way communications system. For example, if a neighborhood person had information, this person would tell the block leader who would inform his or her section leader. That section leader would then call the executive board police contact, and this board member would notify the police. The Civic Association board approved the plan.

My next step was to approach the mayor to gain her support. At that time, November 2001, Susan Bass Levine was the mayor of Cherry Hill, New Jersey, where I lived. The mayor supported the concept, and she sent me to the Cherry Hill chief of police, Brian Malloy, to work out a viable plan

After being thoroughly "grilled" by Chief Malloy, he went to the next step and sent me to Captain Mike Morgan to work out the details.

My meeting with Captain Morgan was also attended by police officer Dave Washick, and was very successful. We agreed on a communication system laid out in charts found in Figures 16.1 and 16.2.

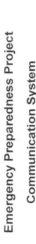
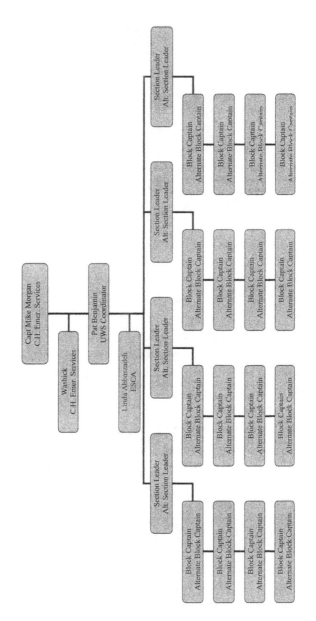

Emergency Preparedness Project
Communication System

Capt Mike Morgan
C.H. Emer. Services

Wastuck
C.H. Emer. Services

Pat Benjamin
UWS Coordinator

Linda Abbaszadeh
ESCA

Section Leader
Alt. Section Leader

Section Leader
Alt. Section Leader

Section Leader
Alt. Section Leader

Section Leader
Alt. Section Leader

Block Captain
Alternate Block Captain

Block Captain
Alternate Block Captain

Block Captain
Alternate Block Captain

Block Captain
Alternate Block Captain

11/20/2002

First Page of Cherry Hill Emergency Preparedness Communications System

Erlton South Civic Association

Emergency Preparedness Program

Role of Communication System Section Leaders and Alternate Section Leaders

1. In your section, replace Block Captains and/or Alternate Block Captains as needed (For example, if they move or resign or for whatever reason can no longer act as a Block or Alternate Block Captain) and notify Project Leader.

2. During emergencies, act as communication liaison between Block Captains within your section and Project Leader

3. Provide Project Leader information given to you by your Block or Alternate Block Captains.

4. Act as communicator to and for residents on blocks where there is no Block or Alternate Block Captain.

Role of Communication System Block and Alternate Block Captains

1. Monitor homes – If a new person/family moves into a home on your block, notify them of our program; have them fill out a data information form; notify and turn in form to Project Leader.

2. If a resident on your block needs emergency help, notify your Section Leader who will notify the Project Leader who will notify authorities. If time is of the essence, notify authorities directly, and let Section Leader know the facts.

3. During an emergency, act as communication liaison for your block to Section Leader who will report to Project Leader. As information becomes available from the First Responders, your Section Leader will provide you with the information and you will pass the information along to the residents.

Second Page of Cherry Hill Emergency Preparedness Communications System

Once this system was established, we began to fill the spots indicated on the chart. The response from the families living in Erlton South, Cherry Hill, was overwhelmingly positive. We sent out forms for people to fill in with information which would help should an emergency occur. Our initial contact produced approximately 250 completed forms, out of 500 families living in the neighborhood. This is a 50 percent return, while my past marketing experience showed that normally this type of contact produces only a 1 to 5 percent return.

Ross Perot helps move us forward

At this point, December 2001, I spoke with Russ Verney (former RPUSA chairman) about my idea for a nationwide organization following the format at the local level that I had laid out with the officials in Cherry Hill. Russ suggested I contact Ross Perot.

Mr. Perot was very supportive and helped the program move forward. He suggested I meet with members of the current administration in Washington DC to inform them about a citizen volunteer network that would be readied to work with the government, to reach out and help prepare American citizens for any future emergencies.

After that telephone call, I began to contact former members of the Reform Party that I could depend on to actively help with this new activity. The initial group included: Donna Donovan of Connecticut; Ira Goodman of New Jersey; Paul and Donna Truax of Texas; Diane and Alec McKelvey of Michigan; Russ Verney of Texas; my husband, Milton Benjamin; my son, Michael Benjamin; and me.

We all agreed to come together at my home. We would address what was needed to move forward with the organizing of a countrywide emergency preparedness network called United We Stand (UWS).

But first came the trip to Washington DC, suggested by Ross Perot.

On January 31, 2002, Donna Donovan and I met with Ruben Barrales and Duncan Campbell from the president's newly forming homeland security team. The meeting was quite positive, and Donna and I were encouraged to continue our work. We were then sent to meet with Steve Garrison, White House deputy on domestic policy, and Karen Marsh from FEMA. They were part of the team responsible for the overall planning of national security.

Rather than exchanging useful information, this meeting seemed to be geared toward picking our (Donna's and my) brains. We filled them in on the meeting with Barrales and Campbell; reviewed our local preparedness test project in Cherry Hill, New Jersey; presented our plans to write a handbook on the threats and methods of meeting these emergencies; discussed the training of all Americans in emergency preparedness; explained the volunteer structure of our new nonprofit corporation, called United We Stand: An Emergency Preparedness Network (UWS); and provided them with innovative ideas on how to address various security issues.

During the meeting, both Karen and Steve took copious notes. However, at the end of the meeting we were not encouraged to continue. In fact, we were told the government had everything under control. They politely thanked us for our interest and information, and we never heard from them again.

United We Stand is organized

While we were meeting with federal government representatives, we were also beginning to build our new emergency preparedness organization United We Stand (UWS). We held our first organizing meeting on February 2 and 3, 2002, at my home in Cherry Hill, New Jersey. The agenda included addressing the legal requirements, the mission statement, role of the national team, training needs, the roles of the state leaders, overall structure, and outreach plans.

Our next meeting took place on March 16 and 17, 2002, again at my home. At that meeting we began detailing the plan to build the organization. First, we decided to write a training manual that could be used in every state by each state leader. In addition, we wanted this manual to be a stand-alone handbook that could be used by any organization or individual American in order to prepare for natural disasters or a terrorist attack.

Along with a training manual, we agreed to organize a UWS Emergency Preparedness Conference for the summer of 2002. This timetable meant the book had to be completed by mid-June, and we had to appoint state contacts and set up the agenda, schedule, location, and date of this conference. We were too naïve to realize that completing these tasks in four months was nearly impossible. We believed it had to be done—so we just did it.

The Emergency Preparedness Handbook

The book was designed, written, and edited by the initial group that helped begin this organization.

First came a letter from Ross Perot encouraging people to get involved. The letter was followed by acknowledgments and thanks to the people who had helped put this manual together—Ross Perot, Diane and Alec McKelvey, Donna Donovan, Paul and Donna Truax, Dror Bar-Sadeh from North Carolina, Russ Verney, Ira Goodman, Ida Terry from Kansas, my husband, Milton, and my son Michael Benjamin from New York City.

The following is the table of contents for the United We Stand Emergency Preparedness Handbook:

UNITED WE STAND
EMERGENCY PREPAREDNESS HANDBOOK

Prepared by Citizens for Citizens

"Everything that is really great and inspiring is created by individuals who labor in freedom. Albert Einstein

Table of Contents

"Territory is but the body of a nation. The people who inhabit its hills and valleys are its soul, its spirit, its life. - James A. Garfield

We shall be judged more by what we do at home than what we preach abroad. John F. Kennedy

EMERGENCY PREPAREDNESS FOR CITIZENS

"If you expect people to be ignorant and free you expect what never was and never will be. Thomas Jefferson

1. When the Media Calls
2. Training and Retaining the Volunteers
3. Questions Volunteers Ask

1. Emergency Professionals
2. Town Council and Mayor
3. Meeting with State Officials
4. Questions from Government Officials

First Page of UWS Emergency Preparedness Handbook

Second Page of UWS Emergency Preparedness Handbook

C) United We Stand, 2002

Page of UWS Emergency Preparedness Handbook

The introduction for the handbook was written by Paul Truax, and was titled "A Wake-up Call for America." Paul also wrote the following chapter, which began the training manual, entitled "Setting Up Your State Network." It is presented below in the following excerpts from the handbook.

Setting Up Your State Network

You went to a meeting, and the leader said, "We need someone to organize this state." No one came forward, so you very reluctantly held up your hand. Does that sound familiar? The organizer breathed a heavy sigh of relief, thanked you, handed you a manual, and moved on. Now you are sitting at home with your chin in your hand and wondering, "Why in the world did I do that? I haven't the foggiest notion of where to start or what to do next."

Are we getting warm? First ... stop worrying. Second ... that's what this chapter is about. Third...others who felt the same way have done it before. And finally, you don't do it all in one day. It's tackled in incremental steps, one step at a time. Hopefully, you feel a little better now; so okay, let's get started.

Media

You are in charge of organizing a state. Let the world know, send out a news advisory. A sample news advisory is included in the Addendum. Where do you send it? Everywhere, to every media outlet you can think of. If there are all-news radio or TV stations in your state, be sure to fax them a release. Since all-news stations have to fill up a lot of time, they are constantly looking for interesting items. It's always better to fax news advisories since personnel and email addresses change.

What do you tell the media when they call? Tell the media what United We Stand is about and why you're involved. (Again, see sample in Addendum).

Now may be a good time to talk about what makes the media tick. Most folks think that the media's function is to inform and entertain its audience. But information and entertainment are by-products. The media is in business to make money. Why do you need to know that? Because understanding that is step one in developing a mutually rewarding relationship with the media.

In order to make money, the media must find people and events to interest their readers and/or listeners. If you take the right approach, you can become a resource for them, someone they'll turn to on a slow news day to enlarge their audience, which allows them to increase their advertising rates. It's a simple equation. You help them, and they'll help you.

Here are some additional points. Newspapers and magazines are about the written word. Radio relies on spoken words, and television is all about image. Keep this in mind as you deal with the media. Make ffiends with them - they can be your allies in publicizing your efforts.

Fourth Page of UWS Emergency Preparedness Handbook

Now back to the news advisory. If you've never sent a news advisory before, you may be expecting everyone to call you, but this is very unlikely. If you get no calls, don't worry because somebody will read it and make a mental note to keep an eye on United We Stand and you. If you get one or two calls, you're ahead of the game.

There is a good way to make sure you get called: mention Ross Perot in your news advisory. Mr. Perot has worldwide name recognition, and the press always wants to know what he's up to. Ross Perot is committed to the success of United We Stand. He communicates with officials of the Bush administration regarding homeland defense and emergency preparedness. Mr. Perot will be available for a limited number of speaking engagements through United We Stand. Do you want to "jump start" your state? Invite Mr. Perot to come and speak. No one inspires volunteers like he does!

Keep in mind local media organizations have limited staff. An e-mail can make their job easier. With an e-mail, they only have to edit - even though you hope they won't! So sending BOTH a fax and an e-mail covers all contingencies.

Make it easy for your radio and TV stations to use what you send. Lead off with a short concise statement that can be used as is. Follow with a longer explanation about who you are and what you are doing ... covering the WHO, WHAT, WHEN, WHY and HOW of your news.

Your state Press Association and state Association of Broadcasters is probably located in your state's capital city. Many of these organizations produce a yearly directory of all press and media in your state which may be on the internet. These are great resources, and not expensive.

Also, when you invite the press to an event send a Media Advisory after you have sent your news advisory - include date, place, time, and a schedule of events. If a reporter calls you about the news advisory, make sure the Media Advisory goes directly to that reporter. If the schedule changes or important details change send another update.

Think ahead about what you'll say when someone from the media calls. It is a good idea to mention that:

*United We Stand is a non-political organization devoted entirely to emergency preparedness and does not have any political agenda.

*United We Stand is working with the current administration through the office of Homeland Security.

*United We Stand wants to attract volunteers from across the political spectrum.

The events of September 11th serve as a reminder that we are all Americans regardless of our individual political ideologies. This type of approach is non-threatening and inclusive. You have now done your first news advisory; there will be many more to follow.

7

Fifth Page of UWS Emergency Preparedness Handbook

It's now time to start organizing your state.

Organizing Your State

*Start small and get your feet wet.

*Hold a meeting in your home.

*Invite friends, relatives, neighbors, and spokespeople from the local police and fire departments to talk to the group. They will become your contacts with those departments. If five or six potential volunteers show up, that's a good start.

*You should have a loose agenda in mind, but encourage your guests to ask questions and give their opinions. That type of participation makes the organization "theirs."

It's time to start "brainstorming" - throwing out ideas. No idea is too far out, too silly, or too impossible to achieve. Yes it can get crazy but if you can laugh together, you can work together. It's creative and everyone can participate. No idea should be criticized. Write every idea down. Then review and create a plan of action. The plus is that everyone leaves knowing that they helped create a working plan ... and that now you are all a team.

Try to get someone to volunteer to be the county captain. If more than one county is in attendance, so much the better. In some areas, it may not be practical to organize by county, so use good judgment as to what geographical breakdown will work best for you.

After the tragic events of 9/11, recruiting volunteers will be easier than you think. September 11th filled the American people with anger and fear, but it also did something else. The American people wanted then and still want to do something. And you're giving them the opportunity. While September 11th is the focal point, everyone hopes that nothing like that ever happens again. Remember that emergency preparedness in case of a terrorist attack also works for natural disasters. There are many examples that can be given for any state. For instance, a tidal wave is impossible in Oklahoma, but tornadoes are common. The mission of United We Stand is to involve, organize, educate, and prepare ordinary citizens as an emergency force to save lives.

Now it is time to focus on the volunteers.

The web site http://www.explorecbd.org/tools/June96/structure.html, by Conservation Based Development has some good items about organizing volunteers. Everything at the web site won't apply to what you're doing, but the following does:

"Begin with an informal group. Many non-profit organizations originate as informal citizen groups, which are motivated to tackle an issue of immediate community concern.

8

Sixth Page of UWS Emergency Preparedness Handbook

Citizens may meet around someone's kitchen table to discuss the issue, plan events to raise awareness, and develop ways to educate community decision-makers."

Train Your Volunteers

- To develop a team of competent volunteers, hold a training session at a convenient time and location. Provide ample refreshments, and thank volunteers for their interest in your work. Give an overview of your mission, goals, and projects.
- Explain the need for dedicated volunteers and their value to the group's work.
- Outline the various types of projects or opportunities there are for volunteers. Matching a person's time, interest, and ability to the appropriate project will help ensure a successful relationship with the individual volunteer.
N Play a game to help volunteers become familiar with each other. This will help develop group spirit and provide the beginning of social relationships, which are often critical to successful volunteer programs.
- Conduct simple role-playing exercises to help volunteers feel more comfortable with certain tasks that they may be asked to do.
- Prepare an information kit and distribute your written materials. This will help communicate your goals and help volunteers spread your message to more people.
- At the end of the training session, have a formal question and answer period so that volunteers have ample opportunity to learn about the organization's work."

Retain your Volunteers

Ten ways to make sure your volunteers continue working with your group:
1. Thank often and with sincerity.
2. Assign specific tasks that may be accomplished within a reasonable amount of time.
3. Explain the purpose of each project and assignment.
4. Provide all necessary materials to complete a project.
5. Train your volunteer supervisor to make everyone feel welcome and at ease.
6. Update volunteers often on the progress of the project.
7. Some volunteers don't work out. Try to reassign, but it is fine to' fire' a volunteer.
8. Make the work as meaningful and as fun as possible.
9. Protect your volunteers from hazards.
10. Recognize all volunteers' contributions. Reward outstanding effort and achievement."

After the first meeting send out a second news release reporting about the success of the event. Include the names of and quotes from those selected as county captains. The news release should include something like; "Jane Smith was selected as county captain of Any County U.S.A. for United We Stand. Ms. Smith stated, ' I'm happy to be of

9

Seventh Page of UWS Emergency Preparedness Handbook

service to Any County U.S.A. and to America.'" Also be sure to mention the names and provide the quotes from the fire and police representatives who attended the meeting.

You've made a good start. Now it's time to go to work on the next county or geographic area. There will be someone who has a contact or contacts in that region. Get the people there to agree to host a meeting. Use the same formula that you used in your county news release, media contacts, etc. By now you know the drill.

You're in for a big surprise. The second one is much easier than the first. The butterflies in your stomach are gone - well, most of them anyway. In fact, you may even be looking forward to it. Would you ever have believed it? If you do your advance work right, a reporter from the local paper will show up. Hey, this is starting to work! As you and/or your representatives move across the state, it will snowball.

It may seem like a long time ago that you sat with your chin in your hand and thought, "I just can't do this." Here's a news flash, not only are you doing it, but it's also turning out to be fun. You're meeting interesting new people, and you're making contacts who might turn out to be life-long friends.

Now you've got the hang of it. It becomes "old hat" to give newspaper interviews and to do radio talk shows as your organization spreads across your state. With each action it becomes easier and easier.

There is a truth that people respect and admire other people who do things because they need doing. You saw a need, and you are filling it. You deserve respect and admiration. You earned it.

Questions Volunteers Ask

You've set up the organization and alerted the press. Now come more questions.

The following questions frequently are asked by potential volunteers, as well as the media. United We Stand leaders from around the country have provided answers. The tone and style of the questions and answers vary because these leaders come from widely diverse areas. Keep in mind not all answers apply in every section of the country.

Question 1: How do you keep volunteers available and participating during times when no real emergency is occurring?

Answer A: First: UWS updates skills annually; for example with refresher courses in areas requiring accuracy, skills and knowledge (e.g. CPR, First Aid, Water Safety, etc.).

Second: Provide recognition based on a merit system. Example: one-year pins and fouryear stripes like hash marks on a sailor's forearm sleeve. Each stripe indicates four years of service. Someone with three stripes would have served twelve years.

10

Eighth Page of UWS Emergency Preparedness Handbook

Third: Every six months host a picnic with competing events. Include competition exhibitions of mock emergencies. To start it off, teams (statewide) would participate. Communities can take turns hosting these events. Keep communities involved by giving each of them a chance to participate in and host events. Teams should practice their skills to remain competitive when participating in these events. Teams will send their best to these meets. Teams can practice their skills to remain competitive when participating in these events. They will be improving their ability through these exercises, instead of just relying on knowledge learned in a classroom setting that may never be used. Those who want to continue and improve physical ability skills and knowledge will do so by staying with the program.

Eventually, each community will develop a team that will attend these events intent on bringing home the Flag (a specially made flag for each state) that they keep for six months until the next meet. Each event should include a mystery mock emergency that challenges the team to improve its skills, timing and knowledge. These mystery mock emergencies are not revealed until the competition begins - to more closely simulate a real emergency. These events, using challenges in mock emergencies, keep teams in top form for an actual emergency. The mystery mock emergency format constantly changes so that nothing can be predicted which would give any team an advantage over another. Mystery mock emergencies are designed to depict any emergency that could actually be encountered. The teams respond as if they are in an actual emergency.

Qualified personnel (Chief of Police, Fire Marshall, etc) can perform judging duties. Merits and awards can be presented by the mayor, a celebrity, or local TV anchor person. Local businesses could sponsor prizes for first to tenth places.

After the first year, each state can have their winning team participate in a meet with other states for the national title. Arrangements for the national event can be coordinated through the national UWS organization. National companies would be solicited to sponsor prizes.

The national event would give volunteers from across the country an opportunity to create new friendships based on common interests. The importance of this is that should a community or state suffer a profound disaster, outside volunteers will have added incentives to assist other communities or another state with common borders.

Also, continually adding and training new volunteers by contacting neighbors and friends not already involved, at the very least, replaces those volunteers who move or decide to leave the organization. At best, we increase the number of citizens involved in protecting themselves, their families, their neighborhood, their towns, and ultimately our country.

11

Ninth Page of UWS Emergency Preparedness Handbook

Answer B: Other ways that volunteers can help their communities between emergencies include: building a swing set for a needy daycare center; speaking at schools to encourage volunteering as a way of giving back to your country; working with special needs people; helping in senior centers, etc. These types of activities act as training for an emergency and build community trust with the volunteers, which is vital when a crisis occurs.

Question 2: Will the information I give you about a personal situation in the family such as disabilities - be shared with the government?

Answer: All of the information given United We Stand will be kept completely confidential. The database will be secure and not made available to any government entity - local, state, or national. United We Stand is not compiling a mailing list to be sold or to be used commercially or politically. Specific data pertinent to saving lives may be given during an emergency to inform United We Stand volunteers and emergency management personnel.

Question 3: Who will handle the database of the volunteers?

Answer: Personal information pertaining to you or your family members will be used ONLY on a vital "need-to-know" basis to assist emergency response teams during an actual emergency. The database of all UWS volunteers will be held by and updated by a UWS volunteer from the National Organizing Committee. [Those who are responsible for, or have access to, the database will NEVER discuss any personal information in the database with anyone, including any person whose information is in the database.]

Question 4: What can serve as a comprehensive warning system if community sirens don't work?

Answer: If sirens are incapacitated, the community can be alerted through vehicles equipped with sirens; i.e. police cars, fire vehicles, and ambulances. There should be proper planning and coordination throughout the area to use those vehicles as alternate warning systems. In addition, a network of ham radio operators is also very effective, and if properly organized, neighbors can go door to door.

Question 5: If there is an attack tomorrow, what steps should be followed?

Answer: This is a great question because it goes to the heart of why United We Stand has been created. Once every city, county, rural area, and state has been properly organized, this question will no longer exist. The volunteers will have assigned duties and will know exactly what to do. Effective organization and a network of alternate communications will limit the effects of disasters, man-made or natural. Read the UWS Handbook to answer your question!

Question 6: Does age matter?

12

Tenth Page of UWS Emergency Preparedness Handbook

Answer: Absolutely not. There are necessary duties which can be performed by volunteers in every age group - from seven-year-old children to senior citizens.

Question 7: Where can the organization turn for financial assistance?

Answer: Turning to local Chambers of Commerce or having private businesses contribute forges community ties. For example, if United We Stand needs a brochure published, a corporation can be asked to "sponsor" publication of the material, and its corporate name displayed prominently on all sponsored materials. [See the fundraising section of the UWS Handbook.]

Question 8: Can United We Stand receive monetary contributions, and are those contributions tax-deductible?

Answer: UWS is a non-profit-organization. All donations are tax deductible. You may mail donations to United We Stand, P.O. Box 87, Colon, MI 49040.

13

Eleventh Page of UWS Emergency Preparedness Handbook

Another pertinent chapter from the handbook deals with "Cities Over One Million In Population." It focuses on New York City and was written by Michael Benjamin, who lived there in 2001. The excerpt follows.

Cities Over One Million in Population

Most large cities have well-organized emergency management systems. These systems are set up, as they should be, to coordinate emergency workers. Individuals living and/or working in large cities are usually left to rely on the media for information. This is not enough to guarantee the safety of as many people as possible. One reason citizen volunteers are needed is to fill the communication gap between the emergency services departments and the citizens of the city.

How can large numbers of volunteers be organized and what role should they play?

Each state volunteer leader in UWS will decide how to organize their citizen volunteers. FEMA (See Addendum for the ICS Course) has an Incident Command System that all state organizers and volunteers should be familiar with since volunteers will be expected to assist in an emergency under this system.

What role should citizen volunteers play?

One critical role of the citizen volunteer is to disseminate information to other citizens living and/or working in the city. Different emergencies warrant different responses, based on as much accurate information as possible. The accurate information must flow in both directions; between Emergency Management services and those people living and/or working in the city, and from citizens to those managing emergency services. The state and city leaders would get as much infort-nation from the emergency services people as possible, and also gather infori-nation from the citizen volunteers via their leaders regarding the situation on the ground at the scene of an emergency.

Now that the civilian volunteer leaders have all of this information, what do they do with it?

One critical focus in an emergency situation is to make sure that everybody is on the same wavelength and working together. The citizens and emergency services need to be following essentially the same plan. The volunteer city leaders need to be in constant communication with emergency services, passing along information to them received from citizen volunteers. Together, the UWS volunteer leaders and emergency services participants need to make decisions based on ALL of the information. The state and city civilian leaders will then pass the information to local leaders -- such as orders to evacuate, etc. For this process to function properly, emergency service departments should have one person whose only job is to work with the citizen volunteers.

Also, in a large city, there are many different "neighborhoods". In a large city the word "ncighborhood" has many mcanings. A "ncighborhood" can rangc from a 70-story towcr to a section of the city that has its own version of "Main Street". These "neighborhoods" have different needs in an emergency.

17

Twelfth Page of UWS Emergency Preparedness Handbook

Large towers can be broken down into two types: residential and office buildings. Residential buildings need an emergency leader, which would most likely be a representative of the building management working with the volunteer building leader. Each floor can in turn have one or two (depending on the size and setup of each floor) trained citizen emergency representatives who will be contacted by the volunteer building leader in the case of an emergency and given instructions. In order to communicate with for example seventy (70) people on seventy (70) floors there should be some kind of intercom system set up on each floor. These intercoms would be placed just outside the door of the floor leader(s). Then, if the floor leader is not home, others on the floor can hear the message and act accordingly. Also, the building leader can speak to everyone at once. Another option might be a two-way radio that each leader carries with him/her. This system applies to smaller residential buildings as well.

Office buildings can have an emergency setup similar to the residential buildings but with one or two emergency leaders on each floor and an emergency representative from each company on each floor.

The key is one person will be responsible for decisions and directions and speak through a communication chain. These directions will be communicated down the line until they have reached all people in the building.

In most large cities, Emergency Service departments are broken down into districts, or precincts. There should be one civilian leader per precinct/district, all the way down to one civilian leader per block.

There are numerous details involved in preparing for the worst. Below are some suggestions based on the actual experience of one of our volunteers in New York City on September I Vh and the days and months that followed.

NEW YORK CITY

New York City consists of five boroughs. Because of the geographical layout, each borough needs its own emergency plan. For instance, the people in downtown Manhattan escaping the collapse of the World Trade Center (WTC) had one certain option; go uptown. Once they were a few blocks north there was the option of going over the bridges, such as the Brooklyn Bridge. There was also the option of the Staten Island ferry. However, once the towers collapsed that service was suspended. In the case of Brooklyn and Queens there was the option to head out to Long Island. People in the Bronx could go north into Westchester. The best option for Staten Islanders was to go over the bridges into New Jersey. But, Staten Island, like Manhattan, is an island unto itself and the big issue on Staten Island was and still is the possibility of all of the bridges being closed. You could neither get out of or onto Staten Island through the entire event, as well as into Manhattan the next day. For situations like that it would be helpful for

18

Thirteenth Page of UWS Emergency Preparedness Handbook

schools to have emergency plans to house children overnight if necessary. Parents should also have a contingency plan for such situations.

In the days after Sept. 11th, public transportation returned to nearly non-nal outside of the World Trade Center (WTC) area. The only public transportation allowed downtown in the few days after were express buses from Staten Island and Brooklyn. The buses were allowed to enter Manhattan through the Brooklyn Battery Tunnel. The Manhattan side of the tunnel is about three blocks from the WTC. Downtown was engulfed in the smoke and dust from the buildings collapse and the burning fires. Many dangerous substances such as asbestos and lead were in the air. As the buses came out of the tunnel the ventilation systems were left on and the outside air filled the buses. I was on a bus and suggested to the driver that he speak to his supervisors about having the buses turn off the ventilation systems until they were clear of downtown. This suggestion apparently resulted in Just that. For the next two to three weeks the bus drivers turned off the ventilation systems as they came out of the tunnel. This example suggests if you see something that would dictate some type of action, by all means make suggestions such as these. This is a great way to make a difference as an individual. This issue of ventilation also applies in the case of biological warfare. If there is a biological attack on a large city, there should be a plan to shut down all ventilation systems in buildings and on public transportation, be it buses or subways.

Another issue is evacuation of buildings in the vicinity of a situation like the World Trade Center. When the first plane hit Tower One, the occupants of Tower Two were told that the safest place was in the building! Many people decided to leave anyway. They were the ones who survived. There was clearly no knowledge of a second plane being on the way to hit Tower Two. But, even if there was no second plane, should Tower Two have been evacuated? Should buildings in the vicinity of such disasters also be evacuated? To answer this question, the following should be asked: How long will it take to evacuate people on the upper floors, be it by the stairs or elevators (should elevators even be used due to risk of power failure)? In very tall buildings, where it can take more than an hour to get down by stairs, it may make sense to begin evacuation. This is obviously dependent on the given situation, but a consideration that can be applied to any tall buildings.

Now, who is to make all these decisions?

A plan by each building's management has to be put into effect, as mentioned previously. One critical thing we learned from the WTC is that command centers should be designated in more than one location. There should be one near the disaster area if at all possible. Of course, there does need to be some kind of post in the affected building from which information can be sent to the main command post where the decisions are being made.

A perfect example of the need for an emergency plan for each building occurred at a building across the street from the WTC a few months after 9/11. The building management announced that there was a small fire in the building and that it was under

19

Fourteenth Page of UWS Emergency Preparedness Handbook

control. One person turned to a co-worker and asked, "When is the last time we heard that?" When someone asked if people should evacuate the building, the employees were told it was up to each individual whether or not he/she wanted to leave the building! No single person was in place to make decisions during an emergency, as is called for by FEMA'S Incident Command System. This demonstrates how important it is that citizen volunteers are prepared to take action to protect themselves and those around them.

Remember, for 72 hours you may be on your own. Never forget what we learned on 9/11, *United We Stand!*

20

Fifteenth Page of UWS Emergency Preparedness Handbook

Also included in the book is a chapter showing how to successfully work with your government and, as a separate insert, tips for working with the media. This chapter was written by Donna Donovan for UWS state leaders.

At the same time, I attempted to find a publisher for the book so that all Americans would have some direction on how to prepare for an emergency, but I was unsuccessful.

However, the time and effort put into preparing this book was not wasted, as we were able to use it at the UWS State Leader Training Conference which took place at the Turf Valley Resort and Conference Center in Ellicott City, Maryland, on July 13 and 14, 2002.

United We Stand Conference preparation

While the handbook was being written, edited, and packaged, we were also preparing for the July 2002 UWS State Leader Training Conference.

We already had contacted possible state leaders and were confident we would have about forty states represented. Then, I contacted one of our active leaders, Micki Summerhays from Oregon. She was a professional travel agent and agreed to help with travel and event arrangements. She was paid a minimum fee for her work.

The next issue we addressed was where to hold the conference. Then, we had to find the cheapest method of getting the attendees to the location. Micki did a great job of locating the airport where the airlines provided the cheapest airfares from anywhere in the country. This turned out to be in Baltimore, Maryland.

Many people, especially along the east coast, would be able to drive. Other state leaders could take Southwest or American Airlines, as well as United Airways, at a reasonable round-trip fare.

Once we had chosen the airport, Micki began to look at the possible places in the vicinity of where we could hold the event. She gave me the name of the Turf Valley Resort and Conference Center. I contacted them and found it was a privately owned hotel with a golf course, located right in the middle of horse country, in Ellicott City, Maryland. It was about an hour and a half from my home, so I drove down there to visit the premises. This looked like a wonderful choice. There were enough rooms for all of our guests, the food was delicious and plentiful, and the cost was reasonable.

We had the location, the conference center, and the attendees. Now it was time to set the agenda for the two-day forum. We decided to focus on training the state leaders and invited a couple of outside guests as well.

The conference agenda

On Saturday morning, July 13, 2002, the meeting was closed to everyone except the state contacts. Paul Truax from Texas discussed "Organizing your state." Reviews of the organizing methods and needs of the state leaders are covered earlier in this chapter, excerpted from our handbook, "Setting Up Your State Network."

Early Saturday afternoon, we welcomed fifty attendees from over forty states. I presented methods of recruiting and training the state volunteers. Training issues revolved around structure, matching the skills of the volunteer with the skills needed for a job, and satisfying the desires of the volunteer as well. In fact, later presentations raised many training issues that would be addressed as each state leader began setting up his or her organization.

We ended the Saturday session listening to Russ Verney suggest fundraising ideas. Russ also discussed how to handle the administrative needs of the state organizations.

On Sunday, July 14, 2002, we started at 8:00 a.m. with a presentation on internal and external communications given by Donna Donovan. Donna had included in our manual a three-page insert titled "Tips for working with the media." For example, Donna had a few suggestions such as, "Always take your mission seriously ... never take yourself seriously," or, "If you don't know the answer to a reporter's question, the appropriate answer is, 'I don't know, but I'll do some checking and get back to you.' And make sure you do get back to that reporter."

When Donna completed her presentation at 9:30 a.m., I introduced our next segment—working with the government.

Our first government speaker was Cherry Hill police captain Mike Morgan, who handled local government emergency management in a town of approximately eighty thousand citizens, which during the day grew to two hundred fifty thousand when additional employees entered our town. Captain Morgan presented a detailed, down-to-earth account of how the Cherry Hill system worked. He took many questions after he finished. In fact, several people approached me after Mike's presentation. They told me how lucky I and other Cherry Hill residents were to have such a great emergency management leader who understood the importance of communication with citizens as well as working with trained volunteers.

After Mike spoke, the next presentation was made by Elizabeth DiGregorio, the FEMA liaison to the White House for Citizen Corp. Citizen Corp was a part of the president's initiative under the umbrella of the Freedom Corp. Citizen Corp brought together volunteers and first responders in a community to find ways to make a community safer and better prepared for all emergencies. Ms. DiGregorio was responsible for developing the national strategy for Citizen Corp and for overall coordination of the program's implementation.

Like Captain Morgan, Ms. DiGregorio presented an honest overview of how we could work with our state and local governments and how volunteers fit into the scheme. It was an interesting exchange between Ms. DiGregorio and the state leaders. Anyone listening was able to get a sense of how different the emergency preparedness needs were in each state. For example, hurricane and flooding questions were asked by people from Florida, North Carolina, and Missouri, while fire and earthquake questions were raised by those living on the west coast, particularly California.

It also became clear, after hearing both Captain Morgan and Ms. DiGregorio speak and listening to the audience issues, that building a rapport with local and state government agencies was not going to be easy. In some places, first responders viewed volunteers as a "nuisance," while other groups were happy to have the help. The people chosen to work with the government needed to be aware of this issue and develop strategies before an actual problem developed.

Finally, we closed the conference with our inspiration—Ross Perot. He spoke about many items and once again raised our awareness and motivated us. But, the part of his speech that still stands out in my mind, five years later, focused on the numerous areas of vulnerability to terrorists that needed to be addressed by the federal government, such as ports and the public water supply.

The conference was a complete success. The food was great, we learned a lot, the people were once again a community and family, and we had a mission to accomplish.

We never anticipated the obstacles that would be placed in our path which would eventually doom the mission.

Volunteers in action

As state leaders returned home to address the structuring issues, the "national leaders" addressed fundraising.

Since I had been successful in setting up a program in the Erlton section of Cherry Hill, New Jersey, we decided to try this in another state and raise funds by charging for our services.

Russ Verney suggested we start with Virginia. He referred me to Randy Flood, who is a former lobbyist and Democrat. Today, he is a committed independent.

Randy is now (in 2007) working with Native Americans to establish a television-training center in Washington DC where Native Americans could develop television production skills. In addition to working with Randy, I was contacted by Mr. Gil Minor from the company Owens & Minor, located in Virginia. This company distributes medical services and equipment to the health care industry.

At first, I had many telephone conversations about United We Stand (UWS), the emergency preparedness network, with both Gil and Randy. Finally, in early 2004, I traveled to Virginia to meet with them.

Randy and I hit it off immediately. We were on the same track politically, and we were both interested in issues, specifically emergency preparedness. We decided to try to work together to exchange contacts and possibly raise funds for UWS.

The meeting with Gil Minor also went well. Mr. Minor strongly supported citizen participation in emergency preparedness through universities and with counties and towns. In fact, he made a call to a Virginia county official suggesting he meet with us. I set up a meeting for Randy and me with the county official. This county administrator was excited by the prospect of having UWS run a conference on training citizens for preparedness during an emergency. I came back to New Jersey excited and ready to prepare a conference agenda.

However, we needed another visit to a possible Virginia location where the conference could be held. Diane and Alec McKelvey, from Michigan, went with me. The location was a wonderful horse farm with a conference building. There were also rooms and cottages where the presenters could stay, and a wonderful dining room.

Finally came the actual preparation of an agenda for the conference. The agenda included a Hazmat specialist, a professional police canine trainer with his bomb-sniffing dog, a well-known keynote speaker, two panel discussions, and a presenter from the federal government to discuss county and town funding for homeland security.

Politics rears its ugly head ... again

The executive director of the three-county Regional Commission, which would sponsor this event, met with us, and later with the county commissioners. At that point, local, county, and federal politics became the flies in the ointment. First was the "not-invented-here" syndrome, meaning since it wasn't their idea they were not about to accept it. Next came the fear that this citizen's initiative, which was out of the "control" of the federal government— or any government for that matter—might take off and turn into a political powerhouse, which could lead to the formation of a third party and become competition for the present two-party system.

Government officials and politicians could not let that happen—and they didn't. We were told that time was needed to make a decision. Guess what? After a year of negotiations, we never heard from them again.

Citizen activists don't give up

We continued to try to raise money. However, people at all levels of government were afraid of the impact this type of citizen's organization would have on their re-election as candidates for the two major parties because, as mentioned above, this organization might lead to the formation of a national alternative political party. These views made fundraising almost impossible.

But we didn't give up.

The next step was to get involved in our town emergency preparedness organizations, and many of us did. I joined the Community Emergency Response Team (CERT) in Cherry Hill, New Jersey. This group is funded by the town, which gets money from state and federal homeland security and emergency management agencies. The larger the town group and the more volunteer participants the town can document, the greater the funding.

However, as I noted earlier, local and state government first responders need to recognize the skills of community volunteers, and how to work with them. If training is not ongoing and these trained volunteers are ignored or not utilized during emergencies, many will leave the group. This will hurt citizen emergency preparedness. In addition, lack of any emergency management initiative can be a killer, as was demonstrated in New Orleans during hurricane Katrina. If an emergency preparedness program had begun in New Orleans after 9/11, and if volunteers had spread the word among their neighbors, the chaos may have been greatly reduced and many lives saved.

Citizens must get and stay involved

The information and personal stories in this chapter demonstrate that citizens and volunteers do make a difference. But, the government officials and workers must learn to accept this fact, and not see it as competition or a threat to their jobs. In times of trial or downright disaster, everyone's help is needed. Also, citizen volunteers need to respect the trained professionals and follow their lead.

Together, elected officials, government workers, and citizens can make our country, states, counties, and towns safer. Alone, we will fail. United we stand together and we will succeed.

Chapter 17

"The price of freedom is eternal vigilance."

Thomas Jefferson's words, above, are the basis of our democracy. In 1992, Ross Perot and his active supporters invigorated the American people. We increased citizen participation in the governance of this country by using several of the following methods of vigilance:

- Organizing and/or contributing to an issues organization, such as: United We Stand America, Habitat for Humanity, the Red Cross, the Salvation Army, and later, a citizen-run emergency preparedness network (the Community Emergency Response Teams—CERT)
- Starting and building an alternative political party, in our case, the Reform Party
- Supporting independent or alternative party candidates for political office
- Writing Letters to the Editor
- Working with lobbying groups such as: Common Cause, Federation for American Immigration Reform (FAIR), League of Women Voters, health care reform organizations, and charter school or voucher support associations
- Requesting or organizing town hall meetings
- Writing articles or books on the issues that matter
- Listening to, and calling in to, television and radio talk shows that cover critical domestic and international problems

- Taking part in the development of up-to-date school teaching curricula at all levels of education, including elementary, middle, and high school, as well as college-level courses
- Creating curricula that address political and government improvements
- Using the Internet to communicate opinions, discuss our country's problems, and introduce new solutions

What went wrong?

Today, the political system is inundated with extremists—from both the right and the left. Some of our elected representatives are self-serving. Some are even corrupt. The American people are now angry or apathetic. Even among our citizens, extreme emotions rule regarding issues, our election system, and our government.

In 1992, we in the reform movement, along with Ross Perot, addressed the issues that really mattered to people. We fought apathy by waking up millions of Americans and getting them to participate in an election campaign and then get out to vote. We tried to channel anger into action. Why didn't we succeed?

As I mentioned at the beginning of this book, the seeds of failure of this movement were unwittingly built into the 1992 presidential campaign. Because it was a presidential campaign, without the underpinnings of state and local races, there was no opportunity to build a real foundation for the movement at the local and state levels. In order to build a long-lasting organization, there should be candidates running for office in every state and, if possible, in every city and town. In 1992, all eyes were only on the top prize—the presidency of the United States.

In addition, the national campaign leadership had to be hastily cobbled together. There was not enough time to seek qualified people who had the skills to continue and to expand a dynamic movement that could anticipate and adapt to a changing, often hostile, cultural and political environment. There was no time to find and train people who truly believed in the issues and ethics for which Ross Perot stood. There was no time to marginalize or exclude self-serving individuals and hangers-on.

However, we were given a second chance to build and grow when Ross Perot created United We Stand America (UWSA) in January 1993. The organization was definitely more structured than the 1992 campaign, but there were still problems. Again, national people took the lead, rather than developing at the ground level (town, county) and building up. There were leaders at every level who did not have the skills needed to organize and run a volunteer organization. In addition, there were many volunteers who were participating for the wrong reason— to meet their own needs rather than those of the citizens as a whole. Even with these weaknesses, UWSA grew to have millions of members.

Then, in 1995, due to pressure from fourteen UWSA state organizations, United We Stand America seemed to go by the wayside, as a new alternative political party took its place—the Reform Party. Once again, the focus was on the United States presidency. Many of the same mistakes that had occurred during Perot's 1992 independent run for the presidency were unintentionally repeated, such as lack of focus on building a party foundation by running candidates for office at the state and local levels. Also, new problems developed as people with their own agendas (such as self-promotion rather than promotion of the issues, or an interest solely in making money) joined the party.

Problems first surfaced because of the eight million votes earned by Ross Perot and the Reform Party in the 1996 presidential election. This vote count qualified the party for over $12 million in matching funds from the federal government, to be used for the next presidential election in 2000.

The phrase "follow the money" aptly sums up the unfortunate story of the Reform Party. Our qualifying for this significant amount drew the notice of Democratic and Republican politicians (including Pat Buchanan), as well as others wanting to get their hands on what they saw as a windfall. Many Reform Party members believe that people from the major political parties joined their party to take over control and get their hands on the money, and eventually destroy the organization. In some circles they'd call this "politics as usual." And who's to say that isn't what happened?

One lesson we in the Perot-inspired political reform movement learned from this experience was the need to train local, state, and national leaders to spot destructive or agenda-driven people and to ethically and carefully structure the rules of the organization so that these "users" can be kept from leadership positions.

Again, not having the time or people with the right skill set contributed to the successful takeover of the Reform Party by Republicans and cashing in by Democrats, like those who sold themselves as convention specialists. In fact, when the "former" Republicans could not get into or take over the existing state organizations, they had created second state "Reform Parties" and applied for formal affiliation with the national party. They also tried to use the politicized court system to gain power and control.

Once more, lack of time due to the 1996 run for the presidency, and the upcoming 2000 election, created the need to bring existing alternative parties and organizations into the fold of the Reform Party in order to quickly increase the membership and voters. The need for speed brought in more self-serving types as well as those interested in the money, rather than our issues and ethics.

Another mistake was not focusing on long-term goals. Short-term goals, such as finding candidates to run in elections, drove the process, rather than the long-term goals of creating a self-funding and self-perpetuating organization.

Ross Perot's goal had always been to get American citizens involved and heard by their elected officials. In order to meet that goal, time and self-funding was and is needed to build a foundation that will support the growth of a successful and durable organization.

External reform movement problems

Even with an internally strong alternative political party, candidates from these parties will not be elected in sufficient numbers until changes are made in our existing election system.

For example, consider ballot access. As discussed in chapter 7, it is almost impossible for alternative parties and independent candidates to either get on the election ballot or to get a decent location on that ballot. The major parties control ballot access and placement and clearly want to enhance chances for the election of their candidates.

In addition, politicized judges and courts usually ruled, and continue to rule, in favor of those people who help them get their job, which means Democrats and Republicans.

These same Democrats and Republicans run the "private bipartisan" Commission on Presidential Debates. They set the bar for entrance into the debates so high and evaluate candidate performance so subjectively that all candidates, except those in the two major parties, are kept out of the presidential debates. This exclusion from the debates then prevents those candidates from communicating with and educating the voters on their stances on the issues.

Another problem was (and still is) the use of "bare knuckle" politics. Within the two major political party structures, negative ads are becoming more the norm than the exception, and the media is used to spread negative news about the opposition. The political parties in control—again, through the media— attack alternative parties and issues movements. In addition, threats and intimidation are used to scare people into backing off and giving in to the rules set up by the two major parties. Many of us in the Reform Party experienced this when the people outside of our reform movement came in to take it over.

Attempts were also made internally, as well as externally, to use lawsuits as a method of intimidation. For example, in late 1999, a lawsuit was filed against the still-serving Reform Party Executive Committee by the Ventura-supported Jack Gargan and Ron Young. We were accused of not releasing information to the newly elected officers, who had still not officially taken office. The process server for that lawsuit came to my door while I was on a business call to California. My husband politely told the man I was tied up with business, and he would take the service. The process server said no, that he would wait until I was finished with the call. He then moved to the sidewalk in front of our house and called the police. He told them, falsely, that my husband had threatened him, and he asked that a police car be sent over to our home just in case he was attacked! Oddly, within minutes of that call, the process server had a heart attack in front of my home. I was never served, and frankly I was not intimidated by this tactic, but many other people in the reform movement were driven away from our group by experiences like this.

Along with these raw political maneuvers, we had to deal with a self-interested media that tried to marginalize the impact of the reform movement and alternative political parties. Think about it. Running a newspaper, magazine, or television or radio station is a business. Therefore, it stands to reason that the owners are careful not to criticize advertisers, which include the major political parties. Use of the words "small," "big-eared," and "wacky" were and still are employed by the media, as well as Republican and Democratic Party stalwarts, to marginalize Ross Perot and his movement in people's minds. In fact, recently I saw a Letter to the Editor in which a writer was supporting Ross Perot's stand against NAFTA, and even this writer called him "small." A person or group which operates outside of the system and has the financial resources—and succeeds—intimidates the establishment. This was clearly the case with Ross Perot, and the media was used to ridicule him and to stop the reform movement he invigorated.

Finally, the issue positions held by Ross Perot and the reform movement were seen as a threat by much of the establishment. For example, in the early 1990s, we were against the passage of the North American Free Trade Agreement (NAFTA). This position, if accepted by Congress, would have hurt the bottom line of large corporations who wanted the cheap labor available in Mexico so they could compete with foreign manufacturers.

Another threatening issue was that of term limits, which clearly would diminish political control by any individual, group, or party.

The issue example that most people are familiar with is campaign finance reform. Politicians within the system, like John McCain and Russ Feingold, tried continually during the 1990s to get a reasonable campaign finance reform bill passed. However, that bill was eventually stripped of the most important reforms before it passed. And now, already in 2007, it's clear that most people running for the presidency (possibly including John McCain) from both major political parties will forego federal funds because of the limits placed on the amount of money they can spend on their campaign. In fact, the current estimate is that $1 billion will be spent on the 2008 presidential campaign!

In addition, our attempt to reduce the influence of special interests and increase the influence of Americans citizens has produced negative attacks on Ross Perot and activists in the reform movement. For example, union officials and members liked our anti-NAFTA stand, but the teachers union had a problem with our support of vouchers, charter schools, and home schooling. Insurance companies were not happy with our support of patients and doctors making the treatment decisions, rather than those who control the money.

Finally, most people, regardless of their position, do not react well to change. They usually choose to remain in their comfort zone. However, when their pocketbooks are affected by rising prices, their children have a problem at school, their medical bills triple, and their property or income taxes increase beyond their ability to meet these payments, their anger finally surfaces. This anger needs to be channeled into action; the way mine was after September 11, 2001.

What about the future?

Identifying past problems and mistakes can lead to a better future. In fact, Thomas Jefferson, along with stating that vigilance is needed to sustain democracy, also recognized another important principle when he said, "If you expect people to be ignorant and free, you expect what never was and never will be."

Today, most people get their information from cable and/or network television news and late night shows, like *The Tonight Show with Jay Leno* on NBC or *Late Show with David Letterman* on CBS, plus programs on Comedy Central, like *The Daily Show with Jon Stewart* and *The Colbert Report*. For many, the Internet is their primary news source. For some, print media—newspapers and magazines—still provides the "facts," although their numbers of readers are diminishing. A 2006 survey by The Radio Television News Directors Foundation found that, across every age bracket, Americans got the lion's share of their news from national and local TV news—more than all other sources combined (*2006 Future of News Survey*).

Part of Perot's legacy was—and is—encouraging people to get involved in their government. However, to accomplish this goal, people need to hear the truth about their government and society. They need the entire picture—not just the good or the bad, but both.

United We Stand America (UWSA), the issues organization started by Ross Perot in January 1993, was an attempt to address the goal of providing the public with a vehicle to impact their government. To the extent that it was successful, it can serve as a model for the future. To the extent that it failed, it will serve to steer us away from making the same mistakes again. Now, we are ready to move forward.

A call to action

In order to spread the information and facts about our government, and continue the Perot legacy, we need to construct a durable, self-funding organization. We need to continue to educate the public so that the people can have constructive input into our political system and have a continuous and lasting impact. We need to provide a vehicle for people that turns anger into action.

To meet these goals in a politically hostile environment, consider the following strategic model for building a successful, strong, and lasting organization:

- Initially, a small group of dedicated and skilled people is needed to build the organization carefully, starting at the local and state levels and using one or two states to test this model.
- The new organization should not depend on only one person at the top. The goal is to build affiliates in all fifty states. Once the foundation has been laid, a representative in each state who has strong leadership skills should be chosen. A fifty-member board made up of these state representatives can be then formed. Between meetings of the board, a small executive committee and an executive director can handle the daily activities of the organization.

- At first, and as the organization grows, its national leaders need to recruit the best talent available. Recruiters of this talent should have the personality and skill-set to identify qualified people to lead the states.
- The structure and rules of the organization should be written in such a way as to exclude or marginalize self-serving individuals, hangers-on, and defined succession process should be in place to ensure the continuing success of the organization.
- The organization's national and state leadership has to communicate effectively with its diverse membership segments, from teenaged people to thirty-year-olds to fifty-year-olds to retirees, octogenarians, and so forth.
- Strong, effective, and continuous communications between national, state, and local components of the organization, both up and down the command chain, is a must.
- Mechanisms need to be put in place to support input from leaders, staff, volunteers, and the public.
- Each leader running a component of the organization has to be fully trained to effectively carry out her or his role.
- For the short term, at least one of the initial leaders must be someone well-known and respected, with start-up capital available, in order to achieve success.
- For the long term, the leaders must build a well-organized and structurally sound organization, with a strong fundraising arm.
- The organization's leadership must have an in-depth understanding of the strengths and weaknesses of a self-serving, and possibly corrupt, political establishment.
- Information regarding strategy and tactics should not be publicized.
- The organization leadership has to strike constructive compromises between opposing forces and should promote itself through this process.
- Organization leaders should understand the operation and requirements of the media so as to provide information to them which furthers the group's agenda.
- Accurate material and facts need to be appropriately packaged for the public and made available to the media for presentation to the people.
- Remember that the media is a business that needs to provide readers, listeners, and viewers with factual information.
- Organization leaders should use technology to further the agenda. For example: high-definition TV and Internet channels; Internet blogs; wiki's; special Web sites; video games created to teach the political process in a democracy, such as *A Force More Powerful*; and other interactive activities which appeal to different age groups and demographics.

These are just some of the requirements that need to be met in order to create a long-lasting organization of individuals who will train the leaders and educate the public. This organization will allow people to have an active voice in advising their government and helping to elect qualified representatives.

Also, this model can be used to build an alternative political party by those who believe the best way to have an impact on government is to get their own candidates—who mirror their points of view—elected to office.

The creation of this type of organization is definitely achievable. Until this organization is up and running, people can participate now by getting involved in the suggested groups and individual activities listed at the beginning of this chapter.

Ross Perot has said many times, "We [the American people] need to take our country back."

The tools to retain a free and democratic country with an involved citizenry are there for the using—or just waiting to be built.

What are you waiting for?
You *can* change the future!

And remember the quote by Sir Winston Churchill that appears above the entrance to Ross Perot's office complex:

Never Give In.
Never, Never, Never

Epilogue

"I cannot tell you how much you mean to me."

On October 12, 2012, in Dallas Texas, **Ross Perot** spoke those words to the people who attended the twenty-year reunion of Perot's run for the presidency in 1992.

When **Margot Perot**, Ross's wife, spoke at the reunion, she said

"I'll always remember your kindness... We were bound together in a common cause and we will always feel bound to you...Nobody told you how to do it and what to do – and you did it."

What we did in 1992 — despite the media bashing fueled by the Republicans and Democrats —was to support and work with Ross Perot to get his name on all 50 state ballots, and help him earn over 18 million votes for the Presidency of the United States.

We — Perot's volunteer army — drew attention to the closed, privately run Presidential Debate Commission, which was established by and is composed only of Democrats and Republicans. Why did they "disqualify" Ross Perot from the debates in the 1996 presidential race? Because Mr. Perot had won the debates in 1992! And since then, no Independent or alternative party candidate has been allowed onto the same debate stage with the Democratic and Republican presidential candidates.

We, the volunteers, along with Ross Perot, brought public attention to: the growing deficit and debt; the need for campaign finance reform; term limits for our representatives in Congress; educational reform; an improved healthcare system; and more candidate choices in elections.

Sad to say, but doesn't this sound a lot like the issues we still face today?

So, who are these people who were lauded by Ross and Margot Perot?

The 2012 Perot reunion in Dallas, Texas was attended by: 1990s volunteers and staff of Perot's 1992 and 1996 independent and alternative party Presidential runs; active members and staff of United We Stand America (Perot's issues organization (1993-1995), with 10 million dues-paying members); and the staff and activist volunteers of the political party started by Ross Perot in 1995 – the Reform Party.

Originally, Perot supporters came from all political perspectives – left, center, and right. However, we were tied in our opposition to NAFTA – the North American Free Trade Agreement -- which has led to the outsourcing of jobs and a huge reduction in US manufacturing.

Where are these Perot supporters leaning politically today?

Kathy Siebel, Tennessee

An early Perot supporter, Kathy was a Democrat. She watched and heard Ross Perot's speech on C-SPAN at the National Press Club, and immediately called his secretary "….and said he should run for President and to take my name and number if he wanted to organize."

Kathy was a county coordinator, and held various other positions in the 1992 campaign. Then, after United We Stand America (UWSA – an issues organization) was formed by Ross Perot in January 1993, she became county coordinator in UWSA, and state chair of the Tennessee Reform Party in 1995. She joined because of her fear of the direction the US was taking with excessive spending, foreign policy, and foreign trade (NAFTA).

Today, Kathy is a Republican-leaning Independent, who says, "I no longer recognize my father's Democrat Party." As we talk in 2012, her biggest concern is "national security, of which debt and economic survival are components."

She's become "…more conservative constitutionally, fiscally, and socially." And states, "I believe there is a place for government, but it has grown too big and is devouring resources."

Brian Nylaan, Michigan

Another Perot activist is Brian Nylaan who has been following politics since he was in the fourth grade. [Me too, and I'm originally from Michigan also!!] As Brian says, "Ross was the siren call I responded to." He states, "My interest and commitment grew after seeing the passion Ross showed after losing a race he could have won, and his pressing on with United We Stand America." He continues "I joined the movement because Ross was the only political leader who at that time wasn't swayed by special interests while focused on fixing our country first." Today, Brian considers himself a progressive "who believes in taking care of people on our shores first." He wants "leaders who will create a level playing field to allow everyone a chance for success." Brian believes that E3 (energy, environment, economy) are the most critical issues that need to be addressed for the future of our children and grandchildren.

Linda Cordero, Connecticut

Linda was an Independent, and not politically active until she watched Ross Perot on Larry King Live in February, 1992. She then went out gathering petition signatures to get Ross Perot's name on the ballot; set up local meetings; and met with others across the state of Connecticut. Linda stayed active after the 1992 election, becoming Connecticut UWSA State Chair in 1993.

Today, Linda is still an Independent, but not active at all. She says, 'I became very discouraged with the way the parties treated Perot, and don't like all the rhetoric from career politicians who don't produce results.'

Linda attended the 20-year reunion and says she "would love to see the billions of dollars spent on campaigns put to good use to benefit the American people. It seems hypocritical for politicians to talk about cutting budgets…and then waste all that money." She believes that "…TV and radio, newspapers and websites should donate equal time for all candidates for two weeks prior to the election."

Robert Davidson, Colorado

Another reunion attendee was Bob Davidson, originally from Connecticut and now living in Colorado. Bob is a self-described political Independent. Bob spent 32 years in the Army, and served under the Army Special Forces Command. Today, his main issue is equality and fair treatment for every American citizen. He is an African American who expressed concern with "the vagueness and changing social and economic stands of 2012 presidential candidate Mitt Romney." Bob says his political decisions are not based on race, but on lack of a clear picture of how Mitt Romney would lead this country.

Charles Kincade, Louisiana

An Obama supporter today, Charles Kincade, a lawyer from West Monroe, Louisiana, was not able to attend the reunion due to court conflicts. But he says, "No one was/is a bigger Perot supporter than me." Charles participated in both the Perot 1992 and 1996 Presidential campaigns. He considered himself a liberal, and still does. "That said, I don't believe anyone -- except Perot -- voiced the central problem with our government, i.e. it's for sale to the highest bidder. Both parties are beholden to well-financed special interests, with the average citizen left out of the mix." Commenting on the 2012 election, Charles says, "To me, there's no comparison between Obama and Romney. Obama is clearly superior. But neither party will address the fundamental issues raised by Perot, the central one being the corruption of the political process." He continues, "I can still hear Perot speak about the need for government to come 'from' the people, not 'at' the people, and how we must assert ourselves as owners of this country."

James Smith, Mississippi

A long time political activist from Madison, Mississippi, James played an active role in the 1990s movement, and was also involved in some local campaigns "in high school and college." Jim was "...always a fan of Ross. Sort of a business hero. When he said he would run if we put him on the ballot, I called Dallas the next day. I was the volunteer coordinator, the campaign director, and UWSA State director." Jim joined to "...draw attention to our spending problems AND to go after the 'head of the snake' in Washington DC by electing a president that would not be a part of the 'system.' " When James was asked what had changed for him politically his answer was "Not a *&@% thing ☺"

Shar Johnson, Michigan

Another Michigan resident, Shar Johnson, who was able to attend the 2012 reunion along with her daughter Heather, was a Republican-leaning Independent before joining the Perot political movement in 1992.

Shar had "...followed Mr. Perot for many years [before 1992] and was...impressed by his straightforward approach to problem solving. I knew he couldn't be bought which meant he didn't need to worry about 'pay-backs'. "

Today, Shar is an independent who is "...a fiscal conservative and socially moderate, who votes based on the issues that most concern me and the character of the candidate." She is "...concerned that the far right is jeopardizing abortion rights, stem cell research and marriage equality for gays, and...fears that the far left is leading us down the road to complete dependence on government. "

Heather Johnson O'Grady, Virginia

Shar Johnson's daughter, Heather Johnson O'Grady, raised in Michigan, is now living in Virginia with her husband and children. Heather was 17 when her mother got involved with the Perot political reform movement. She helped her mother gather signatures to put Perot on the ballot in Michigan, and has tremendous respect and admiration for Ross Perot. Heather and the rest of us still remember the huge decorated cake Shar baked and presented to Ross to celebrate his birthday.

Edward Chlapowski, Texas

Another Perot activist who attended the 2012 reunion, Edward Chlapowski, was an inactive political Independent before Perot appeared on the scene in 1992. Now, Ed believes the Democrat and Republican parties simply have no solutions to today's problems. So, he is affiliated with the newly revived Reform Party. And Ed, along with many political activists across the country, is working to rebuild and turn the Reform Party back into an effective political alternative.

Judy and Steve Lockwood, Washington
Judy and Steve Lockwood, who also attended the reunion, became politically involved in 1992. Judy was a Democrat and Steve was an Independent. Today, Judy is a registered Democrat who votes "for whomever I choose." And, Steve stands politically "nowhere." Today, Judy is concerned about healthcare, while Steve is focused on "…saving myself, my wife, and a few close friends." Steve has basically given up, and Judy still hopes for "…someone to fight for the PEOPLE."

Tim Shaw, Pennsylvania
A Republican in his teens in 1992, Tim Shaw, from Lancaster Pennsylvania today and originally from Philadelphia, is a staunch constitutionalist. Tim's first vote for president was for Ross Perot. His concern was that the two-party political system was moving the United States toward world government. In fact, he believes today's economic globalization will be followed by a worldwide political union. Tim thinks the United Nations has never helped America -- in fact has hurt America, and therefore the United States should not be a member. He supports more in-depth discussions during political campaigns and town halls once a week so we can get to know the issue stands of our candidates better. Tim does not believe the government should be contributing any money toward elections. He supports a very limited role for the federal government: defending the American people. And, Tim states, "There is nothing in the constitution that allows for subsidies for corporations."

Elizabeth Christman Danforth, Texas
Another Pennsylvania native, Elizabeth is now living in Texas. She grew up "in a patriotic family." However, before Ross Perot's appearance on the political scene, she admits she didn't even know who the governor of her state was. Elizabeth started as apolitical; became a political Independent; and today is very conservative and more religious. She has moved from pro-choice to pro-life. She says, "Ross Perot taught me to study the issues and the candidates…" before voting.

Pauline Kline, Florida
Pauline Kline also attended the reunion and played a major role in the 1992 and 1996 elections, later becoming active in local politics. Before 1992, she was a Republican-leaning Independent, and today is a Republican "whose heart is with the Reform Party." Pauline is worried about our inability to follow the constitution, and the poor economic condition in which we now find ourselves. She believes the 1990s Reform Party "…had it all…" and

is disgusted with the way we were treated by the media and the major political parties. She still supports ridding our political system of the influence of lobbyists, and mandating term limits for all of our elected representatives.

Jim Brown, Florida

Another Florida supporter, Jim Brown was a politically inactive Independent "…before joining the Perot Movement in 1992." He worked in 1996 as a grassroots volunteer in Florida. He originally joined the Perot movement because "…it was the first time I felt my beliefs aligned with a person running for office. I wasn't extremely Liberal and not extremely Conservative. I fell in between and the Perot Movement offered me that flexibility that the two major parties did not offer." Today Jim considers himself more of a centrist, "…but registered as a Republican to work to change the Party from within until we can get a third party established. My goal is to do to them what they did to us. Get them from the inside!!! I would be considered a Perot/Paulite [Ron Paul libertarian]!!" In fact, Jim ran for office in 2008 as a Reform Party candidate, "…but it was clear to me, after 20 years of working for Reform, that the country still isn't ready for us and we have much work to do inside the duopoly!"

These are just a few examples of the people who supported and voted for Ross Perot in the 1990s. Politically they came from the right, center and left then. Although the group was painted in the 1990s as extreme right by much of the media, we were clearly a mix of people on the political right, center, and left who came together to focus with Ross Perot on the core issues at the heart of the founding of our country – and remain so today.

What has been the longer-term impact of Ross Perot's political reform movement?

In January, 1993, I was told that if I wanted to actively participate in United We Stand America I needed to venture into the then-new world of the Internet, and I did, along with many other cyber-pioneers. This was the beginning of *political activists across this country using the Internet for political discussion*. And, this usage now dominates the 2012 political campaign.

In fact, the *first on-line presidential primary vote was held by the Reform Party* in 1995/1996 when Reformers nationwide cast ballots via computer for Ross Perot or former Colorado governor Richard Lamm.

Also, Ross Perot is remembered for his use of cutting-edge *infomercials and charts* to communicate political ideas to the American people.

The economic, educational, healthcare and political *problems we first identified and raised in 1992* have intensified in 2012 and 2019, and people are once again asking – "Where is Ross Perot?"

In 1999, Donald Trump joined forces with Jesse Ventura to test the waters for a run in the Reform Party Primary. Trump invited many Perot supporters to meet with him in Florida at Mar a Lago, his Florida home. Of course I wasn't one of them!!

After the meeting and further discussions, Donald Trump decided not to run, and in stepped Patrick Buchanan. The rest is history.

Perot's Impact on President Donald Trump

Even though Donald Trump decided not to run in the Reform Party Presidential Primary in 1999, Ross Perot's policies had an impact on the future President. Although Ross Perot's main interest was reducing the national debt, President Trump jumped on the anti-NAFTA bandwagon and the issue of illegal immigration. (See pages 28-31)

Thoughts after the 2012 and 2016 elections

- Fear rather than the economy appeared to drive the 2012 presidential election results: fear of Republican social extremists, and fear of the unknown Republican presidential candidate.
- The country is divided politically, almost 50/50.
- Most incumbents were re-elected.
- Congress remains sharply divided.

How do we solve the problems still facing Americans – a failing economy; a broken healthcare sector; a dysfunctional system of education; elected officials who ignore the voters; politics controlled by money; and a United States foreign policy determined by terrorists?

Now, more than ever, the American people need to raise their voices and demand that both major political parties work together – and with the people they were elected to represent -- to repair the cracks in the American economic, social and political structure.

We need to discuss, organize, petition, and demonstrate in our state capitals and Washington DC. **Americans need to work together**. We must force the people whom we voted into elected office to stop the bickering and start doing what is necessary to get the United States back on track as "…one nation, under God, indivisible, with liberty and justice for all."

And, we must never forget the words—perhaps more applicable now than ever before -- of Thomas Jefferson:

THE PRICE OF FREEDOM IS ETERNAL VIGILANCE.

Bibliography

Armor, John. *Why Term Limits?: Because They Have It Coming*. Ottawa, Illinois: Jameson Books, Inc., 1994.

Barta, Carolyn. *Perot and His People: Disrupting the Balance of Political Power*. Fort Worth, Texas: The Summit Group, 1993.

Black, Gordon S. and Benjamin D. Black. *The Politics of American Discontent: How a New Party Can Make Democracy Work Again*. New York, NY: John Wiley & Sons, Inc., 1994.

Chiu, Tony. *Ross Perot: In His Own Words*. New York, NY: Warner Books, Inc., 1992.

Gans, Curtis. *Voting and Democracy Report: 1995*. "*1994 Congressional Elections: An Analysis.*" Takoma Park, MD: Center for Voting and Democracy, 1995.

Nader, Ralph. *Crashing the Party: How to tell the Truth and Still Run for President*. New York, NY: Thomas Dunne Books, 2002.

Newport, Frank. "Prescriptions for Healthcare from the People." *Gallup News Service*, April 26, 2007.

Ochoa, George and Melinda Corey. *100 Best Trends 2006*. Avon, MA: Adams Media, 2005.

Perot, Ross, *United We Stand: How We Can Take Back Our Country*. New York, NY: Hyperion, 1992.

Perot, Ross. *Not for Sale at Any Price: How We Can Save America for Our Children*. New York, NY: Hyperion, 1993.

Perot, Ross. *Intensive Care: We Must Save Medicare and Medicaid Now*. New York, NY: HarperPerennial, 1995.

Perot, Ross. Forward. *Preparing Our Country for the 21st Century*. New York, NY: HarperPerennial, 1995.

Perot, Ross. *My Life & The Principles for Success*. Arlington, Texas: The Summit Publishing Group, 1996.

Perot, Ross and Pat Choate. *Save Your Job, Save Our Country: Why NAFTA Must Be Stopped—Now!* New York, NY: Hyperion, 1993.

Perot, Ross and Paul Simon. *The Dollar Crisis: A Blueprint to Help Rebuild the American Dream*. Arlington, Texas: The Summit Publishing Group, 1996.

Posner, Gerald. *Citizen Perot: His Life and Times*. New York, NY: Random House, 1996.

Rapoport, Ronald B. and Walter J. Stone. *Three's A Crowd: The Dynamic of Third Parties, Ross Perot, and Republican Resurgence*. Ann Arbor, Michigan: The University of Michigan Press, 2005.

Renshon, Stanley A. *The Clinton Campaign*. Boulder, Colorado: Westview Press, 1995.

Robinson, James W., Editor. *Ross Perot Speaks Out*. Rocklin, California: Prima Publishing, 1992.

Scott, Robert E. *The High Price of "Free" Trade: NAFTA's Failure Has Cost the United States Jobs Across the Nation*. Washington DC: Economic Policy Institute, 2003.

Sifry, Micah. *Spoiling For a Fight: Third-Party Politics in America*. New York, NY: Routledge, 2003.

Teixeira, Roy and Joel Rodgers. *America's Forgotten Majority: Why the White Working Class Still Matters*. Oshkosh, WI: Basic Books, 2000.

Index

L

Lamm, Governor Richard 85, 87
Lawrence, Mark 72
League of Women Voters 167
Letters to the Editor 167
Liddy, Gordon 88
Limbaugh, Rush 88, 92
Linn, Max 134
Lipke Auditorium 96
Lizotte, Andy 133
Lobbying 39, 58, 71
LoCascio, Vince 98
Lockwood, Judy and Steve 179
Long Beach convention. 119, 135
Los Angeles Times 70
Lott, SenatorTrent 65
Love, Nikki 134

M

Macklin, Tom 134
Madsen, Phil 108, 112, 123
Maline, Bob 109, 110
Malloy, Chief Brian 143
Mangia, Jim 70, 85, 90, 91, 92, 97, 100, 104, 105, 109, 113, 115, 129, 132
Marcum, Louise 60
Marsh, Karen 146
McCain, Senator John 56, 71, 171
McCarthy, Senator Eugene 108
McCloskey, Jeff 125, 126
McDonald, Judge Francis M. 139
McKelvey, Alec 63, 116, 131, 137, 150, 146, 147, 165
McKelvey, Diane 36, 63, 64, 82, 86, 87, 97, 108, 113, 115, 116, 125, 130, 133, 135, 136, 137, 138, 146, 147, 165
McLarty, Mack 65
McLaughlin, Tom 111, 112, 113, 120
media 45, 64, 66, 67, 73, 84, 87, 89, 90, 91, 93, 94, 97, 133, 162, 163, 170, 171, 172, 173
Medicaid 35
Medicare 35
Methods of Vigilance. 167
Mexico 72, 103,
Michigan 36, 63, 82, 86, 105, 108, 112, 114, 115, 116, 125, 133, 135, 138, 165
Michigan Secretary of State 135, 136
Minnesota 108, 109, 110, 112, 115, 118, 124
Minnesota Independence Party 115
Minor, Gil 165
Moan, Gerry 113, 115, 119, 124, 126, 128, 129, 130, 131, 132
Morgan, Captain Mike 143, 163
Morris, Bill 102
Morris, Mike 82, 87, 106, 114
Murray, Daniel 116

N

Nader, Ralph 33, 92, 96, 97
NAFTA 30, 31, 32, 33, 34 59, 60, 64, 94, 114, 172, 173
Nashville Conference 100
Nashville Tennessee 98
Natural Law Party 129, 131, 132, 137
Nazi Supporters 117
negative ads 170
Negative Campaigning 39, 57
New Jersey 35, 42, 45, 56, 58, 67, 69, 74, 99, 101, 104, 105, 117, 131, 133, 140, 142, 146, 147, 164, 165
New Jersey Reform Party 98
New Mexico 59, 64, 73, 101, 105
New York 57, 100, 109, 112, 113, 128, 141, 148
Newman, Jim 60
Nike 65
NJRP Board of Trustees 98
No Labels xv
North American Free Trade Agreement 64, 172
North Carolina 105, 115, 128, 147, 164
Nunn, Sam 59
Nylaan, Brian 176, 177

O

Ohio 58, 61, 64, 71, 73, 83, 104
Oregon 104, 110, 162
Orfield, Myron 108
Owenby, Carl 104, 109
O'Brien, Tom 81

P

PACs 42, 46, 67
Patriot News 99, 100
Patriot Party 70, 99, 100, 113
Pelosi, Larry 41
Pennsylvania 58, 71, 89, 90, 105, 109, 113, 125
Perot for President 7, 70, 134
Perot legacy 173
Perot Systems 88
Perot, Margot 175, 176
Perot, Ross 8, 9, 11, 14, 32, 33, 34, 35, 36, 38, 56, 59, 61, 62, 63, 64, 65, 66, 69, 70, 71, 73, 81, 82, 83, 84, 86, 87, 88, 89, 90, 91, 92, 93, 94, 99, 100, 101, 104, 108, 109, 110, 112, 113, 114, 119, 123, 124, 132, 133, 134, 135, 136, 137, 141, 142, 146, 147, 164, 167, 168, 169, 170, 171, 172, 173, 174, 175, 176, 180, 125, 133, 135, 138, 165
Peterson, Pete 65
Playboy 114, 115, 124
presidency 168, 169, 170, 171
President Bill Clinton 65
presidential campaign 168, 169
Presidential Debate Commission 170
Presidential Debates 93, 96, 97
Public Financing 39
public schools 34, 35

Z

Zimmer, Congressman Dick 33
Zschau, Edward 85